Haunted Yorkshire

NICK TYLER

The
History
Press

First published 2019

The History Press
97 St George's Place, Cheltenham,
Gloucestershire, GL50 3QB
www.thehistorypress.co.uk

British Library Cataloguing in Publication Data.
A catalogue record for this book is available from the British Library.

ISBN 978 0 7509 9137 7

Typesetting and origination by The History Press
Printed and bound by TJ International Ltd

Haunted Yorkshire

Contents

Prologue

For years we have been obsessed with stories of the supernatural – tales of ghostly goings-on and things that go bump in the night. We watch, read and recount terrifying stories of the undead for our excitement and enjoyment, and millions of us claim to have experienced paranormal encounters that we firmly believe to have been real.

We all have an opinion and a firm point of view on the subject. Some claim that the stories offer entertainment but nothing else, that they lack substance and that ghosts simply don't exist. Others are seasoned paranormal investigators claiming to have hard evidence of the afterlife, but the evidence they offer is rarely black and white and therefore open to interpretation. Then there are the armchair believers, who love nothing more than watching a scary film under a blanket or reading a spooky book with a cup of hot cocoa, but they would never dream of visiting a haunted house or graveyard after dark in search of ghostly apparitions.

There are literally millions of video clips, voice recordings and photographs, all claiming to offer proof of the spirit world, yet each and every one of them is equally as credible as they are ridiculous. Perhaps it's better that way, for when the paranormal becomes normal, our curiosity dies.

I have studied parapsychology for nearly ten years and after hundreds of investigations, tens of thousands of photographs and video clips claiming to offer hard evidence, hundreds of psychic studies and various experiments, I'm still none the wiser.

It's reasonable to assume that if the afterlife does exist, Yorkshire would almost certainly be home to numerous ghosts, entities and demons. A county laced with so much history would surely be able to leave an imprint on the fabric of time. From its pioneers of engineering to its gruesome murderous past, the raw emotion that this beautiful county houses would certainly be enough fuel for the spectral fire so to speak.

During this adventure, I have discovered the strange, the bizarre, the unbelievable and the terrifying, all accompanied by a rich and vibrant past. Whether you are a believer, a hardened sceptic or just intrigued as to what could really be lurking in the shadows of Yorkshire, pour the coffee, snuggle under your favourite blanket and read on with an open mind, as I recount some of the tales that were handed to me over the years.

I write not to change your point of view or perspective, but simply to pass on these accounts allowing you to make up your own mind. Enjoy the journey as we delve into *Haunted Yorkshire*.

1

North Yorkshire

Workhouse Museum, Ripon

Hush-a-bye baby, on a tree top,
when you grow old, your wages will stop.
When you have spent the little money you made,
first to the poorhouse and then to the grave.

The Archway of Tears at Ripon Workhouse. The last view of the outside world
for many of the inmates as they entered the final destination.

This chilling rhyme was popular during the nineteenth century, and speaks of the natural lifespan of the poor, often ending in the dreaded workhouses around the country, one of which marks the start of our journey around Yorkshire, Ripon Workhouse Museum.

Whilst researching this book I have visited many beautiful locations around Yorkshire, all with a rich, if not slightly macabre, history. One of my favourite places is the beautiful city of Ripon, located within the picturesque rural roads that guide visitors into the city. This delightful location, with its stunning cathedral, cobbled streets and museums galore, almost transports the mind back to bygone times, but amid its rich history and aesthetically pleasing surroundings, reports of paranormal phenomena are rife, with many believing that the residents of times gone by may still linger, long after their mortal lives upon this earth ended.

The whole city is a haven of both legend and folklore, which is added to by the charming artefacts you can find there, such as an enchanting gravestone that reads, 'Here lies poor but honest Bryan Tunstall, he was a most expert angler, until Death, envious of his Merit, threw out his line, hook'd him here the 21st day of April 1790.'

This humorous epitaph was written after the angler drowned within the waters that he fished during his life. To this day, people claim that his spirit wanders the embankment nearby, and his ghostly apparition can be spotted fishing by the water's edge, or reading the comically macabre headstone within the cathedral grounds.

Another paranormal point of interest in Ripon is the Black Swan public house that, in times gone by, had the local blacksmith to its rear. The long-serving landlady, who left in 2017, reported numerous stories of paranormal phenomena within the building, all believed to have been linked to the restless spirit of the blacksmith.

The reason why the old blacksmith is believed to still haunt the Black Swan is unclear, but the numerous reports do make the mind wonder if his soul still lingers in our mortal realm. One guest awoke during the night, screaming uncontrollably and in a clear state of shock. After staff entered the room, the lady claimed to have awoken to see both the blacksmith and his daughter standing by the foot of her bed, watching her whilst she slept.

Another tale tells of a chap on his way to Scotland, who stayed in the Black Swan after visiting friends in Ripon. When he didn't come down for breakfast, the landlady went to check on him, as he'd stated the previous evening that he needed to be away early the following morning. He was found in bed, claiming to have immense pressure upon his chest and neck that prevented him from rising. He even claimed that he could actually feel hands clasped tightly around his throat, despite no one else being in the locked room at the time.

The absolute epicentre of all the paranormal phenomena around Ripon radiates from the Workhouse Museum, located on the aptly named road, Allhallowgate.

This disturbingly, emotionally charged location, is one of the few remaining workhouses that are almost still complete. The gates at the front, also known as the 'Archway of Tears', create the images of depression before one even enters the historic building itself.

To the right are the tramp's cells, dating back to 1877, where the vagrants could enter for a night or two, providing they had not a penny when searched as they were booked in at the tiny desk. Those found with a penny would be tossed back onto the streets.

They would then have to strip naked, before being given the standard uniform made from coarse, itchy material, followed by a piece of bread or a bowl of gruel for sustenance, whilst their clothes were taken away to be fumigated.

The vagrants were then locked in the tiny tramp cells with only a small bed and a potty, known as a guzunder, because it 'goes under' the bed, with only a couple of very thin sheets for warmth in the bitterly cold cells.

The desk at which the vagrants would be booked in and searched prior to their short stay in the workhouse. Those found with a penny would have been tossed back out on the streets.

During the day, they would be expected to work hard with the permanent workhouse residents, assisting in their daily tasks. The rule was simple: if you could stand, you could work, regardless of age or sex, from infants to the elderly.

The permanent residents would suffer the same entry, only they would be taken to the main blocks at the rear of the grounds, men on one side and women on the other. The master's house in the centre would back onto the dining area, the only part of the building that wasn't segregated. Mixing with the opposite sex was prohibited, however; men and women would eat at different times, in total silence.

If you went in with your partner, you would be split up, only to see each other on a Sunday if you were lucky enough to. The same went for mothers with children older than just 2 years of age. They would also be given a bath in one of the two tubs with no taps. The water was filled and shared by everyone using them, ensuring the earlier the bath, the cleaner the inmate.

Everyone had a role within the workhouse and they would literally work their fingers to the bone. The women would cook, wash or fumigate clothes with hazardous chemicals, whilst the men would smash bones for fertiliser, rocks for the roads or take part in the tedious work of oakum picking, the process of unpicking old bits of rope so that the threads could be mixed with tar and used for caulking the joints of timber in wooden vessels.

Everything about the workhouses was designed to make them the end of the road, so to speak. They were anything but an easy ride, and designed so that the inmates understood this prior to arrival.

The cart outside the building would be used to transport the bodies of those who died within the workhouse to their pauper's grave, a tremendously deep hole in the ground that the corpse would be tossed into before the entrance was temporarily covered up. With only a little limestone to aid their eternal resting slumber, upwards of twenty bodies could be laid on top of each other in these disturbingly tragic graves. It would have been a macabre treat when an inmate died, as others would be hand-picked to leave the workhouse for a day and assist in pushing the funeral cart to the burial ground.

The workhouses were places for people with nowhere left to turn: for men who couldn't provide for their families and had no other option than to have their lives changed forever within the depressive walls.

There was such a stigma attached to them that birth certificates were eventually changed from 'workhouse' to an address, in an attempt to stop those unfortunate enough to have been born in these places from being prejudged.

With so many negative emotions attached to places like these, it's little wonder that the Workhouse Museum in Ripon is allegedly home to a whole host of paranormal phenomena. One apocryphal story tells of Harriett Rodwell, who attended the workhouse in the late nineteenth century. Harriett was tired of the life she was leading and decided to tie one end of a scarf to a door handle whilst the other end acted as her noose as she threw herself down the stairwell to her death.

The staircase was bricked up until recently, but there have always been strange reports of a gurgling sound or a thudding noise emerging from the area over the years. Of course, the idea that Harriett would have chosen to kill herself in such a painful way is questionable, as is the mystery of where she managed to get the scarf from. Whether or not the disembodied noises are hers, they are reported from a wide number of visitors with no prior knowledge of the tale.

Another story tells of George Greenwood's first wife. George was the master of the workhouse and as such, his wife automatically became the matron and was responsible for the infants and children. As the story goes, the guardians, who were the people responsible for financing the workhouse, visited the matron and were unimpressed at her lack of fortitude.

The matron spoke with friends at a workhouse in Wales and learnt of their ways of disciplining unruly children. From then on, any naughty boys or girls would be taken into the small room behind the classroom, where they would be locked in the large cabinet for an hour or so as punishment.

One day, an insolent 5-year-old boy was locked in the cupboard when the matron received news that her sister was gravely ill in Leeds. Within the hour, she was on the carriage, so concerned for her sister that she had forgotten all about the poor boy who was still locked in the cupboard.

When she returned some three days later, everyone was looking for the boy, believed to be an escapee. The matron was told that the room behind the classroom had been searched, but not the cupboard. The small boy was then discovered, barely alive, before sadly passing soon after. The matron followed suit just five months later when she died during childbirth.

Her ghost is said to wander the old area of the workhouse to this day, wringing her hands and wailing at her part in the death of the poor young boy who was already malnourished prior to being locked away without food or water.

These are just two of the many stories that are whispered around Ripon Workhouse Museum by the staff, the volunteers and unsuspecting visitors. Ghostly shadows seen wandering around the cells, disembodied voices echoing through the

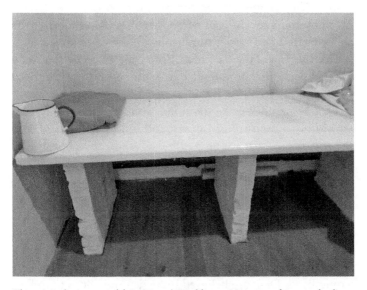

The original mortuary slab in Ripon's Workhouse Museum, where any bodies would have been laid out after death. A place where many claim to be able to tune into the negative emotions attached to the building.

rooms and strange footsteps are also seen and heard on a regular basis. There is undoubtedly the feeling of being watched as you navigate through the macabre setting but is there more than just tricks of the mind within Ripon Workhouse Museum?

Of course, as with all museums, the place is full of trigger objects that can almost transport visitors back to the days in which this was a running workhouse, but does that mean that the ghostly goings-on are simply a case of pareidolia, caused by the suppressed atmosphere of such a sad place? Or are the restless spirits of the Workhouse Museum at Ripon truly haunting the place to this very day?

Knott Road, Ryedale

Located in the North York Moors National Park, Knott Road runs towards Hollins Lane and then further on to Rosedale Abbey. The phenomena on the road itself is often overshadowed by the generic tales of ghostly monks wandering the abbey nearby, but the actual remains are not of an abbey at all. In fact, they are of the Cistercian Priory, the difference between the two being that nuns resided in a priory whilst monks lived in an abbey.

That alone does make the mind wonder if all ghostly tales are simply a mixture of history and folklore that fuse into the apparitions that we hear of today. Whilst the ghostly tales of monks in this area are sure to be stories that have been fabricated over the years, there is another strange phenomenon that is regularly spotted here: a ghostly pack of large dogs that wander the rural lanes from Knott Road to the old Cistercian Priory.

It's important to differentiate between these beasts and Black Dogs, as they are in fact different phenomena altogether. The iconic Black Dogs are believed to be demonic dogs from hell, said to snatch the souls of sinners before dragging them down to their fiery damnation. Other variations suggest that they can offer protection in the way one would expect a guardian angel to do so. Both aspects are showcased in the Hall Lane tale in the West Yorkshire section.

'Ghost dogs' or 'ghost packs', on the other hand, are not demonic at all. They are spectral apparitions, often sent to guard a specific location. They are frequently believed to be the afterlife's version of reincarnation, as the souls of the nuns were transformed into these strange entities to guard the remains of the old priory.

The folklore that surrounds these mysterious beasts is ambiguous at best, but it appears that they rely on fear to warn away people from a certain location and are not actually capable of physically attacking humans.

There are many stories that corroborate this theory, as the ghostly animals regularly snarl, bark and chase unsuspecting travellers, but they have never been reported to get within a biting range, let alone attack a human.

As the legend goes, these animals have guarded the area ever since 1535, when King Henry VIII's dissolution of monasteries caused the building to be torn down. The little that remains of the old Cistercian Priory is now guarded by the ghostly hounds, preventing further damage being caused.

There have been many sightings of the creatures over the years and they are usually described as Alsatian-type dogs with dark brown hair and eyes and, unlike the Black Dog, their hair is described as being short and they often appear in ghostly form with a vague transparency.

The pack has been spotted around the old priory area on numerous occasions, but they are most commonly seen on Knott Road, which would have led visitors down to the Cistercian Priory in times gone by.

Reports commonly include the pack of around eight to ten beasts, running out in front of cars during the evening, or snarling and barking fiercely at anyone walking or cycling along Knott Road. The ghostly barking of the pack can be heard echoing around the area throughout the night and has often been mistaken for wolves, although there are no wolves roaming the area any more, despite many of the local place names deriving from the packs that would have stalked the forest in times gone by.

As with any woodland road, it is beautiful by day and eerie by night. With that being said, it's possible that domesticated animals may escape and roam the area whilst following the scents from other animals within the boscage. It would, however, be unlikely to find eight or ten escapees all at the same time.

On the other hand, the sightings could have been of wild animals such as badgers or foxes that, under the cover of darkness, were mistaken for dogs. Could it even be that a simple story of a single animal that was spotted in times gone by became more as the tale was recycled and retold?

Or perhaps, a 'ghost pack' really is roaming Knott Road, their ghostly howls warning people against further damage to the old Cistercian Priory and protecting this remarkable piece of English heritage for eternity.

Becks Brow, Wigglesworth

The B6478 between Wigglesworth and Tosside has been the unfortunate location of numerous fatalities over the years. Like so many other similar tales, a combination of speed and driving conditions are often to blame.

Between the heartbreaking fatalities, however, there are tales from people who have crashed upon this stretch of road and lived to tell the tale. Some of these stories, despite only being a small percentage, tell of another possible cause of the accidents on Becks Brow.

It is said that the full-bodied apparition of a White Lady materialises along this stretch of road, particularly on dark and damp nights. She is believed to be the lost soul of Leanne Walker, a 21-year-old who was tragically killed in the late

1970s when her boyfriend lost control of his car on this stretch of road, killing them both instantly.

Since that fateful night, there have been numerous sightings of the White Lady, often walking by the side of the road or standing still on the grass verge and looking around for her boyfriend, almost as though she's unaware of the sad fate that befell her.

Some motorists claim that the spirit actually runs out across the road in front of their cars, causing them to swerve and lose control themselves. Others say that the mere sight of her was enough to break their concentration in the damp conditions.

I set about searching for any eyewitnesses who could corroborate the tale and stumbled upon Michael Bell. Michael was travelling back to his home in Tosside on the night of his experience. Following suit, he said it was dark and very wet when he encountered the phantom that ended with a trip to the hospital. This is his story:

It was back in April 2011 when I had my accident. It was a really bad night, the rain was literally pouring down and the roads were treacherous. I wasn't going too fast because of this as I made my way along Becks Brow.

When I got to the bend, I saw what I thought was a woman, standing soggy wet through by the side of the road. I've never in my life stopped to pick anyone up but I pulled over that night because of the weather. As I stopped and looked back, she'd gone. I called out for anyone but there was no answer.

After a few moments I put it down to my imagination and carried on driving back towards Tosside. As I drove around the next bend, I saw the lady again. Only this time she wasn't standing still. She was sprinting along the side of the road. I was so confused that I didn't even realise how far past the sighting I was and that there was no way it would have been the same woman.

As I slowed down to drive alongside her, suddenly she shot out into the road, right in front of my car. I turned sharply before the car spun out of control. I thank god there were no other motorists on the road at the time. I careered off the lane and into a tree where I stayed for a moment getting my bearings.

Then the excruciating pain in my chest and leg came through, but I was able to grab my phone and call for help. I suffered a broken leg and severe bruising from the seatbelt but other than a few scratches, I was otherwise okay and thankful every day for that.

I never for a second thought I'd seen a ghost but now I've heard the story I can't help but wonder.

Michael's terrifying account is like something straight out of a horror movie and if true, is the most violent account I've encountered given the injuries he sustained, despite them not being directly inflicted by the spirit.

You might argue that his account was little more than his imagination. You could suggest that the medication he received to numb the pain may have been responsible for the memory he's created. I was so intrigued by the tale that I decided to delve a little deeper into the story and there was one significant factor that I uncovered.

On that night in April 2011, Michael was tested for alcohol as is the standard procedure at all road traffic accidents. His test was positive; he was nearly four times over the legal driving limit. I discussed this with him, but he maintained that he was of perfectly sound mind at the time and the apparition he saw was as he described.

Michael was happy for me to use this tale but asked that his name be changed to protect his identity – interestingly, only after being questioned about the alcohol consumption.

York Museum Library

This strange tale dates back to 1954 and tells of a seemingly haunted book. The publication in question was regularly found on one of the tables as staff arrived for work each morning.

It was said to have been about conspiracy theories and was always open on a different page as though it was being read by an unseen presence. There wasn't anything remarkable about the volume; it wasn't overly popular nor a best seller in its day. It was just one of many books within the library that gathered dust until such time that someone was intrigued enough to read it.

The janitor at the library decided to keep watch one evening and stayed through the night, watching the shelf that housed the old book that was moving so often.

At around 4.00 a.m., the janitor claimed to have seen the full-bodied apparition of an elderly gentleman wander through the library to that very shelf. He was said to be dressed in trousers and a knitted green jumper with the collar of his shirt showing the black tie he donned over the V-neck.

As the janitor watched on, the spirit carefully took the book before strolling over to the same table that it was found at each morning. He sat quietly, unaware of the janitor who was keeping watch over the spectre, and read the pages with a hearty smile, thoroughly enjoying each page.

After around an hour or so, the janitor watched on as the elderly gentleman slowly vanished into thin air, right before his eyes, the book being left open on the page he was reading. He wanted to pick the book up but thought it better to wait for the staff to arrive and share the account with them.

Not only did they all believe his spooky tale, but numerous members of staff also claimed to have seen the same apparition wandering the library during the day, although at the time they didn't know he was a spectral being.

None of the staff kept a look out after that night, but it was said that the thick book was still found every morning on the same table, each time a little further on in pages.

Shortly after the janitor's account, the book finally reached its end and on 9 October 1954, it was found on the table, closed and rear side up. That was the last time any of the books were disturbed during the dead of night.

This is a wonderfully charming story and it does make the mind wonder: did the elderly gentleman start the book whilst living out his twilight years, the cruel hand of fate ending his mortal time on earth before he could finish the pages?

With the theory that ghosts can remain in our world long after they are dead, it's an interesting point of view that perhaps they remain for their own reasons. Perhaps missing loved ones and wanting to watch over them isn't the only reason that spirits visit.

Perhaps, like the elderly gentleman in York's Museum Library, they simply started a book in life that they didn't get to finish, and visit from the afterlife to see how it concludes.

Grape Lane, Whitby

Whitby is infamous for its literary tales of vampiric beings said to reside in and around the historic seaside town in North Yorkshire. The ruins of Whitby Abbey, overlooking the North Sea from the cliff top, were in fact said to be Bram Stoker's inspiration for his famous novel, *Dracula*.

But it's not just the vampires that visitors need be wary of; Whitby also has scores of alleged sightings of the undead wandering its streets at night. So many so, that the beautiful seaside town is commonly believed to be one of the most haunted places in the UK and has been the setting for numerous other novels and films over the years.

Gruesome tales of horror, disembodied voices, ghostly footsteps and horrific folklore are all commonplace at this location and, amidst the tales of phantom coaches that drive through the streets before disappearing, the oyster man who is said to wander the beach shouting 'come and get your fresh oysters', and the cruel landlady of the White Horse and Griffin Pub, is the strange story of Mary Clarke, a young local girl who died in the most horrific way back in the early twentieth century.

Grape Lane in Whitby.

Mary Clarke was said to have long, flowing blonde hair that she was so incredibly proud of that she brushed it with 100 strokes every morning and every evening. She grew up in Whitby with her parents but, despite her father working, the family were not of means, as was common at the time.

In 1917, her father asked the girl to go to the local bakers to warm his tea up in the oven, something she'd done numerous times over the years as the baker was a close friend of his.

It's worth noting that another version of the tale claims she visited for warmth on a cold evening, but this is less probable as the bakers wouldn't allow people in for that reason with so many paupers around at the time. Regardless of her reason for visiting on that particular evening, she had no idea of the horrific fate that awaited her.

Mary went over to the oven and reached inside to put the plate in but, as she did so, her hair caught fire. Because it was so long it was up in flames in a flash, and the panicked girl shot out of the shop as the baker watched on in horror.

As the wind outside hit the flames, it literally added fuel to the fire and within seconds they had spread onto Mary's clothing. As the baker rushed out to her aid, she was now engulfed in the flames and burnt beyond recognition, the whole street consumed by both smoke and the scent of burning hair and flesh.

The baker fought to extinguish the flames before carrying the charred body of Mary to the infirmary. Her blistered, bubbling skin continued to peel from her bones as she arrived. In an even worse twist to the tale, the nurses at the infirmary discovered that she was still breathing, although unconscious from the pain.

By now most of the skin on her body had burnt and peeled away as the doctors and nurses tried in vain to save the young girl. She was pronounced dead around thirty minutes after arriving at the infirmary.

Ever since that fateful night, there have been many alleged sightings of the poor girl amongst other strange phenomena, including the crackling sound of fire and the smell of burnt flesh. Generally, people will experience any single one of those phenomena, although some have been lucky – or unlucky – enough to have experienced all three at once.

After researching this infamous story, I was introduced to a young woman named Chloe Freeman who had been walking along Grape Lane late one evening with friends. This is her account:

It would have been about half past ten on a Thursday night when we were walking along Grape Lane. We all knew the stories of Mary Clarke because we were all born and bred in Whitby, but we'd never seen anything before and didn't really pay much attention to them to be honest. I thought they'd been made up by the people that arranged the Whitby Halloween stuff anyway.

On that particular night, we walked past that building and suddenly my friend said she could smell something burning. We all sniffed the air and smelt it too. It was a strange smell, not like plastic or rubber but just as disgusting.

At first, we didn't even think of Mary Clarke; we were more bothered about the smoke getting into our clothes and hair. We could only smell it at the time though; we couldn't see any smoke or a fire. Then my friend shouted for us to look back, down the street.

Suddenly, out of nowhere, this burning figure appeared, staring right at us. We could smell the fire and feel the heat from it, as though we were standing by the bonfire on November 5th.

The figure just stared at us, almost as if it didn't realise it was on fire and, at that moment, my friend screamed, 'It's Mary!' and then panic really set in.

We screamed and started running away but as we neared the end of the road, I glanced back only to see the burning figure had vanished into thin air – she was completely gone.

We walked over to the spot where she'd appeared, frightened to death but curious at the same time, but there wasn't anything there. No smell, no marks on the pavement, nothing.

Even now I look back and wonder if we imagined the whole thing, but deep down I know that we didn't. I've never believed in ghosts before that night, but I sure do now, and I'll never walk along Grape Lane at night ever again.

After hearing Chloe's tale, I set about finding her friends. One has now moved to Manchester to study Law and chose not to be involved in the production of this book. I sensed the experience had taken its toll on the young lady and most likely caused lasting effects, although it's equally plausible that she thought her account might hinder her future career options.

The other girl, named Lisa Wilmot, was happy to talk about the experience. Her account was almost word for word the same as Chloe's. The only discrepancy was the location on Grape Lane where the spirit was allegedly spotted. Lisa told me the phenomena had occurred quite a way up from where Chloe claimed it had taken place, right outside the old bakery.

It could have been hysteria that caused the girls' experience on that fateful night. They admitted growing up with the story and therefore were familiar with it.

Perhaps there actually was a neighbour having a fire and, due to their location, they simply conceptualised the whole episode. It's hard to imagine that they would remember the wrong location given the fact that they claimed to have consciously returned to look at the pavement, but that doesn't necessarily mean their account is untrue.

With over fifty other witness accounts of strange phenomena on and around Grape Lane in Whitby, it does make one wonder if Mary truly is replaying her horrific death over and over for all eternity. Or if the numerous other tales of ghostly beings said to wander the streets at night have any truth to them.

Of course, the accounts could also be simple folk tales that have taken on a life of their own as they have been retold. Or perhaps Whitby truly is a paranormal hotspot, with a plethora of undead spirits wandering the picturesque seaside town in North Yorkshire.

Stonegate, York

The strange tale that takes place at what is now Jack Wills in York has something of an urban legend feel attached to it. Previously there was a small changing room at the rear which was used by staff when the building was a different business.

A few weeks before Christmas, Jade Masters, an 18-year-old temp, was checking her face in the mirror before starting her shift. She claimed that she was all alone at the time but as she glanced at her reflection, she noticed another girl standing behind her.

The girl was described as being of a similar age and wearing jeans and a yellow top. Nothing unusual at all. Jade turned to the girl to say hello; as she was only a temp, she wasn't overly familiar with other staff members and figured the girl was someone she was yet to meet.

Jade then stated that she said hello and the girl smiled and nodded at her, acknowledging her welcome before turning and walking away. As she got to within a couple of feet of the door, she turned and walked straight through the wall right in front of the bewildered spectator's eyes.

Jade shrieked in panic and fled the changing room, rushing to tell other staff members who all assumed she was making the story up. She refused to return to work and subsequently lost her job due to the encounter.

On face value, you might argue that she did indeed fabricate the tale, that it was little more than the imagination of an attention-seeking girl. But the story gets even stranger when the history of the place is researched.

The door that Jade used to exit the changing room had only recently been added, the previous door being in the exact location where the alleged phantom walked through the wall. The door was changed for security reasons as it made segregating stock safer for the business.

The original doorway may well have dated back to the building's construction, hundreds of years ago. The phantom's clothing and expression, however, have a much later feel to them, possibly 1980s onwards.

But with no known deaths that fit the bill, no records of any former employees that died whilst working there, who was that mysterious phantom? And if she truly did exist, why was she seemingly getting prepared for work?

It's worth mentioning that despite my research, I've been unable to uncover any other sightings of this alleged apparition, however some people claim to have heard disembodied footsteps, ghostly whistling and the eerie sound of a young woman singing within the old changing room.

Interestingly, another shop just a few doors away tells the story of a young girl who tragically fell to her death on the staircase. Her apparition is said to be spotted regularly, perched in the cabinets in the shop and smiling at people as they enter. On the occasions when she doesn't appear as a full-bodied apparition, her footsteps can be heard around the building along with the angelic sound of her innocent singing.

As this apparition has been seen by numerous people over the years, could it simply be that Jade transferred the details to her own account, whether intentionally or not?

Or perhaps designer clothing is not the only thing residing at that shop on Stonegate in York, arguably one of the UK's most haunted locations.

Newby Hall, Ripon

One of the worst forgotten accidents of Britain was the Newby Hall ferry disaster that occurred on 4 February 1869. On that fateful day, Sir Charles Slingsby of Scriven Park mounted his faithful steed Saltfish, joining various other noblemen as they embarked on the biggest foxhunt of the year in search of the Stirrup Cup.

Charles had been twice defeated in the same location by a fox that chose to escape being mauled by crossing over the River Ure that runs by Newby Hall, located just 4 miles from the notorious Ripon Workhouse Museum. Charles was a proud man and believed it to be the same fox, taunting him as it escaped.

This hunting trip followed suit: a fox was flushed out before making its escape once again over the river Ure. This time, however, Charles and his huntsmen friends decided to outwit the animal by crossing over the river themselves and maintaining their pursuit.

The waters were dangerously high and flowing rapidly on account of the heavy rain that had been pouring upon the region for the previous month, but the group elected to hop onto the ferry that would take them across the river towards Westwick.

Unlike the boats we envisage today, this was little more than a wooden raft that was attached to a chain that, in turn, attached to a cog which could be turned to enable the boat to cross the river. The group made it almost to the halfway point before the spooked horses started stirring up.

The site of the Newby Hall ferry disaster that took place on 4 February 1869.

Saltfish, the most visibly frightened steed, was the first to escape the boat trip by jumping into the freezing water below. The horse kicked out violently whilst trying to stay afloat before becoming entangled in the chains that turned with the cog.

As the other horses kicked out in fright, the already over-loaded vessel became unstable and despite the huntsmen's efforts, the remaining horses began to buck, resulting in both the riders and animals being tossed into the dangerous currents.

Charles attempted to swim for the far bank but was unable to do so on account of his heavy riding attire. After thrashing against the strong current for a few minutes, he became exhausted and submerged beneath the icy cold water, drowning.

Five other huntsmen were also killed that fateful day along with every single horse but one. Ironically it was Saltfish, the original cause to the boat's instability, that managed to struggle over to the bank and scramble to safety.

A stained-glass image of Sir Charles Slingsby is currently in Knaresborough church, commemorating the nobleman and his huntsmen friends who lost their lives on that fateful day.

Ever since the tragedy, there have been tales of strange occurrences around the riverside gardens and the ferry crossing at Newby Hall. Strange light anomalies, believed to be orbs, have been spotted on a regular basis, along with the disembodied cries of men, desperately fighting for their lives, that echo around the night skies.

In 1998, a group of four friends visited Newby Hall when they went out to see the old ferry crossing. They claimed to have seen two gentlemen, dressed in hunting attire, resuscitating a third chap on the opposite embankment. When the friends shouted over to see if they could offer any assistance, the two men looked over at them before all three slowly faded away, disappearing right before their eyes.

Another tale tells of a phantom horse that wanders the gardens before running away into the trees. It has been described as being a black stallion with a white plaited mane. Numerous people have approached the animal that looks as solid as you or I, but whenever they get to within a few feet it dashes away into the woodland.

There are no known wild horses in the area or any locals owning a stallion that matches its description. One can only ponder whether or not the steed is, in fact, the apparition of one of the horses that were also killed on that tragic day.

The tale of Sir Charles Slingsby is common around these parts and therefore you would have to assume that those claiming to have witnessed any kind of phenomena would have previous knowledge of the story which questions their credibility. But does that mean that the strange accounts are untrue?

Maybe the fabricated stories come from attention-seeking individuals; maybe they simply imagine the phenomena that they claim to encounter, or just maybe, the spirits of Sir Charles Slingsby and his hunting party are still replaying the events of that fateful day in the afterlife, as the tragic tale is marked on the fabric of time at Newby Hall.

The Green Lady, Settle

This traditional market town, nestled deep within the pictur-esque Yorkshire Dales, is famed for its local Victoria Cave, an ancient cavity named in honour of Queen Victoria's coro-nation. The historic site was home to such discoveries as the skeletal remains of ancient inhabitants, Roman coins, pottery, fish hooks and jewellery, but if you look past the history that was found in this sleepy Yorkshire town, there is another local legend that takes place here.

It is a gruesome tale of murder dating back to the eighteenth century, a story that is still told to this day and believed to be responsible for the ghostly sounds that echo around the night skies of Settle along with a strange phenomenon known only as the Green Lady.

The folk tale begins with the landlord of the local tavern named Jonathon, and his treasured collection of prized pigs.

When Jonathon wasn't tending to his business, he would spend his time feeding, cleaning and grooming his collection of swine ready for local farmers' fairs.

Unfortunately, Jonathon's passion for his prized pigs was not shared with his wife Rose; she became increasingly jealous of the swine that took up so much of her husband's time.

On the night of their wedding anniversary, Rose cooked up a special dinner for her husband and waited to surprise him when he returned. After a few hours, she was tired of waiting, knowing once again she was playing second fiddle in his life. With the food spoiled, she became enraged, shouting that he'd never treat his beloved pigs in the same manner that he treated his wife.

It was clear he was not coming home any time soon and, as the story goes, she covered the spoiled food in rat poison and carried it out to the pigsty, tossing it in and laughing as the greedy animals gobbled up the feast before them.

Within just a few moments, the pigs started to squeal and fall over as the poison took its toll. As they writhed in pain on the ground, Rose began stabbing at them with a pitchfork, one by one, ensuring her husband's beloved animals were all dead.

Hearing the commotion, Jonathon, who had been drinking all afternoon in his pub, walked outside and followed the ruckus, which led him to witness his wife murdering his prized animals. He was thrust into a blind rage and charged towards Rose, snatching the pitchfork from her before thrusting it into her stomach. As she lay bleeding on the ground, she told her husband that she was pregnant with their first child.

Seeing that his wife was dying, and fearing the repercussions, Jonathon lifted his wife's limp body and carried her to the river where he disposed of her before returning to drink with friends as if nothing had happened. The body was found two days later, but Jonathon was never charged with the murder as his drinking partners refused to admit that he had in fact left the pub that evening.

To this day there are reports of the ghostly sounds of pigs squealing, echoing around the night sky of Settle. Many people have reported seeing what appeared to be a woman, dripping wet, with skin that, at a glance, appeared to be green under the street lamps.

Many locals believe in the Green Lady who is said to haunt the town to this day and it is commonly believed that if she is seen, a family pet will be found dead shortly afterwards.

But is there any truth to this strange local folklore tale or has the story created the suggestion that people expect to hear the ghostly sounds and therefore, the mind creates them?

Perhaps the screams truly are heard, yet they are little more than pigs from neighbouring farms. It seems inconceivable that Jonathon heard the commotion from inside the busy pub, yet he came out alone to check on the noise.

On the other hand, there have been over thirty different claims of the strange phenomena dating back to the 1950s and perhaps there were even more unrecorded claims before that time.

Whether or not the story rings true and regardless of whether or not the Green Lady of Settle is in fact Rose, the eerie feeling you get when investigating the area after dark is hard to ignore and strange occurrences have been reported by a whole array of different people from all walks of life. With that in mind, it does make one wonder, what does hide in the shadows of Settle after dark?

Kiplin Hall, Richmond

Dating back to the seventeenth century, this delightfully charming Jacobean manor house has passed through four families over the years. It was originally built as a hunting lodge by George Calvert, secretary of state to King James I.

As with all old historical buildings, ghostly stories and claims of unexplained phenomena are rife within Kiplin Hall,

Kiplin Hall, Richmond.

and there are numerous spirits said to be haunting the property to this day.

An eerie tunnel linking the north tower with the service wing is concealed behind the walls. This would have allowed servants and maids to travel unseen via hidden entrances in various fireplaces. This spooky passageway is said to be haunted by the apparition of a large woman with a stiff upper lip. Based on her demeanour, it is thought that she would have been the housekeeper during her life and she is said to hurry along anyone dawdling around the tunnel. By all accounts, she does not appear in ghostly form, but instead, she appears as a solid looking, full-bodied apparition that appears so real that many people have mistaken her for an actress.

A gothic style drawing room that is now a library was built in 1820 and is said to have three spirits residing within its four walls. The ghostly figure of a doctor is reported to stand by the old grand piano, looking down upon it with a thoughtful gaze.

A small girl is often said to appear in the room, screaming loudly before vanishing before bewildered spectators' eyes. Finally, the ghostly apparition of a priest that appears in an alcove is thought to be protecting Lord Nelson's chair, an artefact that is still there to this day. He appears looking sternly at any guests in the room before vanishing into thin air.

In the current drawing room, the ghostly apparition of a woman in white is commonly spotted, gazing out of the window looking for someone. This spirit is thought to be the ghost of Elizabeth Carpenter, the mother of John Carpenter, 4th Earl of Tyrconnell, who was thought to have been killed in Russia whilst serving the queen in the nineteenth century, although many historians dispute this.

Amidst the ghostly apparitions that are commonly encountered around Kiplin Hall, many people have also reported the loud cries of a woman during the night, numerous other shadows that approach visitors in what is described as an intimidating way, and loud footsteps stomping around the building.

Strangely, the first alleged sighting of a ghost here was reported back in the seventeenth century, when two maids claimed to have seen the figure of a woman rushing around the servants' wing in what could be the oldest recorded ghost sighting in England.

Victoria Talbot visited the historic building in 2018 and kindly met with me to share her strange encounter:

I was exploring Kiplin Hall with my husband when for some strange reason we got separated. He was looking at the historic objects in the hall, but I thought he was strolling on with me. As I reached the library, I noticed he wasn't there, so I started looking over the beautiful room expecting him to catch up at any moment.

As I explored the room, I heard piano music playing and turned to the grand piano to see a gentleman standing by it. He was wearing what I can only describe as an expensive looking Victorian suit, complete with hat and jacket. I smiled at the man assuming that he was part of the exhibition, before saying hello, but he ignored me. I figured he was in character, so I left to get my husband.

A few seconds later we returned to the room, but the piano was now quiet, and the man was gone. It was only later I realised that no one was actually seated, playing the instrument.

After my experience, I learnt of the ghost stories associated with that room but I never for a second suspected the gentleman could have been anything other than a real man. He was so vivid and solid looking.

The other strange thing was, there was no other way he could have left without coming out of the same door where my husband and I were standing. When I was told of the ghostly goings-on they said I'd encountered the phantom doctor, but he didn't look like a doctor, he just looked like a fella in Victorian clothing.

I really don't know what to make of the whole experience now, but it didn't frighten me. I'm more intrigued than anything else.

As with all buildings of this nature, one would expect to hear stories of alleged paranormal phenomena, and with the preserved look of the old place, suggestion is almost certainly a key factor as the mind jumps to conclusions.

Certain objects can act as triggers to impressionable minds and transport them back to a different time or place. Think of walking into a mortuary and seeing a coffin; you'd immediately become spooked.

The fact the phantom appeared in a suit rather than the doctor's attire that he is normally seen in does suggest that Victoria's mind may possibly have played a part in her strange tale.

The thing that separates Kiplin Hall for me, is the sheer volume of alleged witness accounts by people from all walks of life, all apparently experiencing the same things.

In the absence of any real evidence, it's hard to say for certain if this old building is indeed haunted, although it might be better to tread carefully should you ever wish to visit the picturesque building and beautiful gardens in North Yorkshire, or you might find out what's really lurking in the shadows.

The Phantom Horseman, Hambleton Hills

Cleveland Way, running through Hambleton Hills in North Yorkshire, has long since been the location of alleged paranormal sightings. Witnesses claim to have been driving along the road, often on a dark and damp night, when a horse appears as if from nowhere, before dematerialising into thin air just as fast.

The horse is said to be mounted with the shadowy figure of a male rider, often wearing a feathered hat in a way that casts the mind back to the old highwaymen of yesteryear. Many drivers claim to have swerved and skidded to avoid the steed and rider before getting out of their car to inspect for any damage, only to find no sign of the mysterious apparition.

In addition to drivers, numerous ramblers and cyclists exploring the picturesque Hambleton Hills have also claimed to have seen the ghostly phantom that is said to appear in either ghost form or as a full-bodied, solid-looking apparition.

On occasion, motorists have even called the police, believing that they may have caused the horse to have been knocked into one of the fields next to the road. When investigated, however, no evidence of a collision, other than the occasional tyre mark, has ever been found.

The truly bizarre thing about this encounter is the sheer volume of witnesses claiming to have seen the phantom horse and rider, all of whom are from different walks of life and most of whom had no prior knowledge of the tale. It's also possible that, over the years, there have been hundreds more from people who haven't thought twice about seeing what they believed to be a normal person riding a horse along the rural lanes.

In addition to this stretch of road, the horseman has often been spotted in various other locations around the area, although never in the same volumes as he's spotted on Cleveland Way. Could it be the same spectre? Or is it feasible that there might be more than one phantom horseman haunting Hambleton Hills?

In my search for eyewitness accounts, I came across Louise Colton, a young lady who had recently moved to the area and claimed to have encountered the phantom whilst driving along the stretch of road in 2010. This is her story:

> I was driving along Cleveland Way when I got stuck behind a horse. The roads are narrow and winding, so I was unable to overtake it. The horse and rider looked jet black and I assumed it was because of the moonlight, creating the silhouette image in front of me. At that point, nothing struck me as strange about it.
>
> As I looked for a spot to get by the animal, it suddenly disappeared right in front of my eyes. Strangely, I wasn't scared, I was more confused than anything. I looked over into the fields expecting to see it had actually jumped over the fence, but it wasn't there either.
>
> Feeling puzzled, but still not spooked, I continued driving along the road but after a minute or so, there it was again, walking by the grass verge. I checked my mirrors in case there was more than one on the road, but we were alone. There was no way it could have moved that fast to get so far in front of me.
>
> This time, I didn't take my eyes away and watched intently as I slowly drove behind it. Sure enough, after a few moments, it faded away, once again. It did scare me that time and I drove away along the empty rural road as fast as the conditions allowed.
>
> A week or so later, I told a friend about the strange experience and she told me it was common to see the phantom horseman around Hambleton Hills.

Louise was new to the area, having only moved there one month prior to her strange encounter. Historically, it would be almost impossible to discover the identity of the

Janet's Foss in winter.

phantom horseman, although folk tales romanticise that it might indeed be the infamous highwayman John Nevison who is discussed further in the West Street tale in the South Yorkshire section.

We can only assume that he may have been a traveller or highwayman, who perhaps lost his life here in times gone by. Maybe he had an affinity with the area for some reason, and that's why he chooses to revisit. Next time you find yourself in the Hambleton Hills area of North Yorkshire, keep an eye out; you may see more than the beautiful scenery.

Janet's Foss, Malham

The stunning waterfall located close to Malham village gets its name from a local folk tale that claims that the small cascade is home to Janet, Queen of the Fairies. Over the years the picturesque site has been used for numerous things, from sheep dipping to wedding ceremonies, all conducted with the enchanting air of the legend.

But amid those visiting the magical scene in search of Janet, there are tales from those who claim to have encountered something different: a malevolent entity that feeds off of the life force or aura of anyone unfortunate enough to come face to face with it. Often described appearing as a green mist floating out of the water at the foot of the falls, this rare phenomenon is thought to be that of a wraith.

There are numerous theories surrounding the legend of the wraith; some claim that she would have practised black magic in life and this eternal damnation is her punishment. Others claim that she was a green lady, similar to the legend in Settle, but she became so vengeful, so aggressive over the years, that she turned into a creature much worse.

Generally speaking, wraiths are not thought to be ghosts or demons, but rather a strange entity somewhere in between the two, similar to poltergeists but much more powerful when appearing as a full-bodied apparition.

There have been many alleged sightings at Janet's Foss over the years, and people thought the phenomenon to be Janet herself, which begs the question: did people spot the wraith in times gone by and assume it to be an enchanting fairy?

The Brothers Grimm tales that speak of fairies and such like are in fact dark stories that have been adapted to children's tales over the years. Is the same principle occurring at Janet's Foss in North Yorkshire?

I rummaged amid the ambiguous accounts, before finally meeting two people who claimed to have come face to face with this mysterious entity in recent years. The first was a lady called Joan Potter, a 72-year-old grandmother, visiting the falls with her grandchildren in the autumn of 2014 when an enjoyable family day out took an unexpected turn. This is Joan's account in unedited form:

> We were walking along the footpath towards the falls. It was a beautiful sunny day and I remember the faint smell of garlic was still floating across the air from wild plants in the woodland.

My granddaughters were seven and nine at the time. They'd run on ahead to see the waterfall, and my husband and I were wandering along the path towards them. Suddenly, we heard them shouting to us both excitedly, eager for us to join them. They were screaming that they'd found the fairy in the water and we both smiled at one another as we hurried along the path to the falls. Of course, we assumed they were just excited at having found the waterfall, but we wanted to share the memory with them nonetheless.

As we arrived at the water, we looked on, a little bewildered, as a strange green mist floated over the surface. Every few seconds it seemed to gather and attempt to rise up, before blanketing over the water once more.

We weren't scared at all, as we believed it to be something to do with the atmosphere, the water and the tufa deposits from the calcium perhaps. My grandchildren wanted to paddle and swim, but we asked them not to, for fear of anything in the mist that might be harmful, even though we were confident it would have been fine.

The strange thing happened when my husband wandered over to the side of the water. The mist gathered in the centre, before moving over in his direction and floating upright by him. The children and I thought it was a magical sight, but my husband had a cautious look on his face before he turned and said we had to leave.

He grabbed the children, who were screaming to remain at the falls, and marched off back along the path. I followed, asking him what the matter was, but he wouldn't say. Over the next year he hinted that he'd seen something in the mist, but he never actually gave me any details.

Sadly, he passed just over a year after our trip to Janet's Foss and despite my curiosity, I've never returned since. My husband was a kind, loving man and it wasn't like him to be spooked by anything, especially a little mist on a waterfall. For that reason, I do believe he saw something at Janet's Foss that day, something that only he encountered.

Intrigued by Joan's story, I set about finding any other accounts that could coincide with her tale, and I was introduced to Adam Wilt, who visited the area with his partner Sarah two years after Joan. This is Adam's account:

Me and my partner, Sarah, went for a trip to Janet's Foss as we'd been dating for over a year and I'd decided to propose to her. The beautiful location just seemed like the perfect place. We wandered the woodland, spotting different things along the way. We each put a coin in the money tree and made a wish – mine was of course that she'd say yes to my question.

Shortly afterwards, we arrived at the falls and sat for a while, soaking up the sunshine and admiring the stunning scenery. I remember feeling incredibly nervous at the time and I kept going over in my head how to pop the question. As I'd just finally plucked up the courage, she laughed and pointed over to the water where a strange green light was flickering above it – it reminded me of the old fireflies you'd see on children's cartoons.

Sarah stood up and, after removing her shoes, stepped into the cold water and watched the strange light anomaly. It seemed to spread out whilst losing its glow, before essentially covering the water in a strange green tone. I told Sarah to get out, but she was so engrossed, she ignored me. The green mist then collected in the centre of the water in a kind of ball, before rising up. After a minute or so, it was floating above the water almost like an old statue, covered in moss, I really don't know how else to describe it.

At that point I was petrified, but Sarah just stood there watching on, as the green figure floated over the water towards her. I knew it was time to go, so I grabbed her by the arm and pulled her out onto the bank. The strange thing happened the second her feet stepped out onto the grass: she became hysterical with fear and we rushed away as quickly as we could.

She later told me that the glow was so beautiful and welcoming whilst she was in the water but, as soon as she stepped out, it was like a mask being taken off of the figure and she saw a horrific looking old woman. I didn't see any of this myself, but I believed her.

Adam's story intrigued me, so I set about finding Sarah, who had sadly gone her separate way in life. She was reluctant to speak about the incident but when I read Adam's account to her, she agreed that it was correct to the word and gave her permission for the story to be used.

Both accounts are interesting but give cause for concern when analysed. The young man may have been affected by his excitement on the day, or his sad memories of times gone by with a woman he clearly wanted to spend his life with. Throughout his tale, he repeatedly referred to Sarah as his partner, despite their separation. He also longingly looked on as he recounted one of many precious memories with her.

Joan, on the other hand, was understandably distraught at her husband's passing, and therefore it's possible that her account has been subjected to more details due to confabulation, the term given for people who remember certain details, but for whom the mind creates images and memories to fill in the blanks; a theory often used when people claim to have past life memories. It's interesting that both accounts were not first hand. Could they have been distorted as such?

There are so many other accounts of this phenomenon that it remains an interesting tale. Of course, it may well be nothing more than people imagining fairies, the reason for many a visit. It could also be simple science, the vapour from the water carrying dust from the nearby woodlands creating the image that many people claim to have encountered.

Whatever the reason for these strange tales, Janet's Foss is truly an enchanting place to visit and enjoy – but tread carefully, as you might venture out in search of Janet, Queen of the Fairies, but instead stumble upon an entity far more dangerous.

Busby's Chair, Thirsk

This strange tale is not of ghosts, wraiths or demons, but rather of an age-old legend involving an allegedly cursed chair; a legend that dates back to the eighteenth century and is still believed by many to this very day.

This enchanting story that marks the end of our journey through North Yorkshire begins back in the early eighteenth century, when a drunken failure of a man named Thomas Busby got into an argument with his father-in-law, one Daniel Auty.

Busby was the most unsavoury of characters. A violent temper and short fuse made him a man few would want to upset. There is much speculation as to why the pair quarrelled, but the general consensus is that it would have been a monetary disagreement, as the pair were both involved in the illegal coining trade – the process of counterfeiting coins that was punishable by death. The ruckus quickly escalated and ended with Auty's lifeless corpse being dumped in the constable's stables.

After Auty was reported missing, a search party was dispatched and quickly found the crudely dumped body as suspicion quickly fell upon Thomas Busby. When the police went to arrest the man, he was found slumped in his favourite chair, a position in which he spent the majority of his adult life, whilst working in his illegal trade.

After being tried and convicted of the crime, Busby was sentenced to death by hanging. His dying wish was to have one last drink in his favourite chair. The chair was brought from his home to the gallows and, after sitting and enjoying his final drink, he cursed the chair, stating that death would befall anyone stupid enough to place their derriere upon it.

With his last words having been spoken, he was hanged on site before his soulless corpse was hung on the post or stoop, as it was commonly known, as a reminder for vagabonds to remain within the law.

Following his execution, the local tavern was rebranded as Busby Stoop – now the Jaipur Spice after being converted into an Indian restaurant in 2013. During its years as a public house, the chair was acquired as a novelty item for guests to visit and sit upon, and people would come from far and wide to view this unusually macabre artefact.

The chair quickly grew a reputation of the witchcraft variety as numerous people that came and sat upon it became victims of tragic accidents shortly afterwards, all of which were attributed to Busby's final curse.

The most notable of these ocurred when two Royal Air Force pilots sat in the chair in 1967, only to die on their way home from the pub as their car collided with a tree, while in 1971, a builder sat in the hexed seat before plummeting to his death from the roof of a nearby conversion he was working on, just an hour later.

In 1978, the chair was donated to the Thirsk Museum where it remains to this day, pinned to the wall to prevent further unfortunates falling victim to the curse. But the strange story didn't end there.

A historian, specialising in furniture, examined the old chair and discovered that the spindles were in fact, machine-made, a process that wasn't introduced until 1840, some 138 years after Busby's alleged death. The correct spindles for a chair dating back to 1702 should have been pole-turned and therefore, the chair in the museum could not possibly have been that of Thomas Busby.

This caused the conspiracy theorists to argue that the appraisal was false, given only in a bid to stop further unfortunate deaths. Of course, if that were true, why did the chair remain on show in the museum instead of being disposed of? Interestingly, the historian refused to sit in the chair himself whilst checking over the antique. He claimed that there was no outcome that would have benefitted him doing so, even though he wasn't superstitious. If nothing happened to him the believers would still believe, but if he was to have an accident shortly afterwards, they would confuse the event for being proof of the chair's curse as pareidolia set in.

Others argued that perhaps the Busby Stoop still had the original chair and gave the museum a fake as they didn't want to give up their prized possession, although it seems implausible that the museum wouldn't be able to spot the fake.

After searching for records relating to Thomas Busby's execution, it would appear that the assizes records for 1702 were lost, casting doubt and adding further mystery to the bizarre tale. After considering all the evidence, I believe that the story was fabricated in a bid to bring customers to the pub in times gone by.

Perhaps certain people bought into the legend so much that it almost took on a life of its own, much in the same way that lady luck is defined as a state of mind, rather than an actual presence. You envisage good fortune and therefore you feel lucky and, in turn, prosper. Is this the same? People sit in the chair and expect something bad to happen, causing their minds to make it so?

It's also worth remembering that the majority of people visiting the chair when it was in the Busby Stoop would have consumed alcohol and would most likely have been inebriated. Perhaps this was responsible for the pilot's car crash or the builder that plummeted from the roof.

Perhaps the pub staff have retold the story on so many occasions that they actually now believe the tale, or perhaps, the legend of Thomas Busby is true, and the old chair is in fact truly cursed by the condemned man's final words, and in turn responsible for many deaths over the years. There's only one way to know for certain – take a seat.

2

South Yorkshire

The Hoober Stand, Wentworth

As our journey leads us to the southern part of Yorkshire, it seems only fitting to begin with the infamous Hoober Stand in Wentworth. If you were to visit the picturesque winding lanes of rural Rotherham, you would find this strange monumental building, situated upon one of the highest ridges in the area. Constructed in the mid-eighteenth century, it is one of several decorative buildings marking the end of the 1745 Jacobite Rebellion.

The Hoober Stand itself is a beautiful, yet strange-looking building, offering fantastic views of nearby Wentworth from its peak, which is open to the public each Sunday. Over the years, however, the site on which it stands has often been tied to bizarre occult practices and alleged paranormal phenomena.

The downward hills and slopes offer a stunning woodland scene but if you explore the small area fully, you are sure to find remnants of the after-dark activities that are a regular occurrence here. Altars, shrines, pagan paraphernalia and occult symbols carved deep into the trees are just a few of the mysterious things you will stumble across.

The area is a hotspot for both dark witchcraft and devil worshippers and there are countless stories of people visiting the

The Hoober Stand near Wentworth in Rotherham.

area after dusk, only to be chased away by persons unknown wearing long dark robes.

One such story claims that two young men were exploring the area late one evening, but after stumbling across a small group of hooded figures they were chased out of the grounds and back along the road for a few hundred feet before the mysterious group retreated back to the Hoober Stand to continue with their bizarre activities. The young men were so intrigued that they decided to return the following day to investigate, only to find the carcasses of numerous crows that had been nailed to the trees around the woodland area. They claimed the birds had been gutted and marked in what they could only describe as sacrificial ways.

In addition to the mysterious groups of people using the Hoober Stand for their private activities, other reports of ghosts, witches, orbs and electronic disturbances are also regularly documented here, but what is it about this place that makes it so unusual after dusk? Is there some kind of unseen energy or presence that perhaps draws in these groups of individuals who devote their lives to the dark side of the occult world? Or is it just the eerie nature of the grounds that make it the perfect location for their practices? As none of the groups are willing to discuss their activities, we can only speculate.

I have personally visited this location numerous times with many different paranormal groups and, despite the mysteriously tense atmosphere that is hard to ignore, I've never encountered any phenomena that I believe could not be explained.

Intrigued as to whether this place houses any real spirits, I set about searching for individuals who had experienced strange things here, and was inundated with responses. Hundreds of people claimed to have experienced some kind of paranormal phenomena within the grounds and, amid the tales of ghostly whispers echoing around the woodland, strange knocks on the front door as if coming from the inside, and a ghostly apparition of a tall hooded figure guarding the building on a full moon between 11 p.m. and 3 a.m., I encountered John Anderton, a local paranormal investigator who agreed to meet with me to share his account. This is it in unedited form:

It was the middle of October and I decided to visit the Hoober Stand with two fellow investigators. We'd done so numerous times before, but never really experienced anything

I'd call paranormal. Of course, we'd captured various orbs and other light anomalies on photographs, but with so many trees around it would be impossible to discount insects, flies or dust as the source.

On this particular evening, we parked in the lay-by just next to the entrance and sneaked past the house at the gates. Although it's a public footway, we did not like having unnecessary disturbances whilst we worked, plus we also imagined the person living in that old house would have been sick to death of people causing a nuisance here after dark and didn't want to add to their stress.

The night was much the same as any other before: we wandered the building, looked for any new stone shrines that might have appeared, and photographed the markings on the trees before heading back to the actual building itself. The ground was dark but the building was lit up by the moonlight. I remember it being a clear night but very cold as we could see our breath, which can cause an issue, particularly when trying to photograph paranormal things.

We called out the usual questions: 'Is there anyone here wishing to communicate? Are there any spirits within the Hoober Stand?' But as before, our calls went unanswered.

At about 10.30 p.m., we decided to call it a night as we had to be up early for our day jobs. As we headed back along the woodland path towards the road, we heard twigs snapping from the area we had just left. Assuming it to be animals, my friends wanted to check it out all the same – after all, we'd been there for over an hour without incident, so another five minutes couldn't hurt.

As we walked back to the main door of the Hoober Stand, we heard whispering all around us in the woods and we all stood still, listening intently. The words were all but unintelligible but, as we focused on the sound, my friend called out, 'King James!'

At that precise moment, the whispers stopped and he would tell me later that evening that King James was the only thing he was able to make out. As we slowly edged back towards the woods to investigate, a little spooked but excited also, a strange figure started to appear at the foot of the stand, like a shadow gaining momentum every second.

At first, it looked like wisps of smoke, but there was nothing on the ground that could have caused it. As it grew to be about four feet in height, it started transforming to the clear figure of a man and at this point, all three of us fled the area in fear.

We have returned numerous times since that night but never experienced any other genuine phenomena. I firmly believe that I saw a full-bodied apparition manifesting at the Hoober Stand and to be honest, I'm just gutted that the whole experience spooked us so much that we couldn't carry on investigating.

John's story is certainly a strange one and it does tie in with some of the other similar accounts. The reference to King James is also interesting, as the buildings were constructed to commemorate the end of the 1745 Jacobite Rebellion, involving supporters of King James II.

The time frame also matches up with other tales of a large ghostly apparition patrolling the foot of the Hoober Stand on a full moon. John also stated that although he remembers the sky being very clear, he was unable to remember if it was indeed a full moon that night.

As a paranormal investigator with hundreds of cases under his belt, it would appear to be a genuine account. On the other hand, you might argue it's little more than a fabricated story, designed to bring publicity to his services.

The fact that the group were spooked by what was indeed most likely to have been an animal rummaging in the woodland, combined with the eerie nature of the location itself, could have simply caused a state of hysteria amongst the three men. Perhaps the smoke was in fact little more than dew reflecting under the moonlight.

As John stated he'd visited the location on numerous occasions before, one would have to assume that he'd researched it well enough to know its purpose for being built, and therefore the King James revelation would not be considered at all credible to the story.

Regardless of your own opinion, the witchcraft, the devil worship and the pagan paraphernalia at the Hoober Stand are all points of fact and you may encounter these yourself at any given time. As for whether or not there is something darker than people residing around that old building will always be an enigma.

Gill Lane, Ecclesfield

A house on Gill Lane was allegedly haunted by a rather violent poltergeist back in the 1970s. The family living there at the time were so scared that they moved in with family members temporarily before buying a different house altogether.

It all started with kitchen drawers being opened, over and over by an unseen hand. The mother believed that it was one of the children playing games so didn't overthink the phenomenon before it escalated over the following week.

The family would hear a bang from the living room, only to rush through to the kitchen and find the top cupboard wide open and a single can rolling across the floor. As before, this carried on for a week or so before moving up yet another notch.

The telephone that was plugged into the kitchen socket was violently thrown to the floor by an unseen hand with such force, in fact, that the plastic casing actually shattered into several pieces. The family still refused to believe it was anything ghostly and simply replaced the phone, warning the children from going near the new one in future.

Sure enough, the next day the same thing happened again; the phone was broken into several pieces. The phenomena carried on for a little while longer before coming to a head on a summer's evening.

On this particular night, all the previous things happened simultaneously. The drawers opened, a can fell from the top cupboard and yet another phone had been broken.

This was enough to force them to leave, but what was only to be a temporary measure soon became permanent when a tin of paint was thrust across the room as the family headed for the door. It was said the father ducked just in time, the heavy tin of emulsion narrowly missing his head as it flew past.

As the tin of paint crashed into the wall, it exploded into a shimmer of magnolia paint that covered both the parents and their eldest child. Petrified at witnessing the strange event with their own eyes, the family fled, never to return.

This scary tale has an air of 30 East Drive to it and follows only a couple of years after the violent poltergeist in Wakefield hit the headlines. With that being said, could it be possible that this was an elaborate hoax?

There are two key factors that are worth noting. Firstly, the family had just finished glossing the living room skirting boards and had numerous tins of excess paint spare. It's strange that the single tin of emulsion was picked as the item to be thrown across the room, the difference obviously being that the gloss would have permanently damaged their clothes and the carpets whereas emulsion would have been a lot easier to clean up.

Secondly, the phenomena stopped once the family moved out and weren't repeated in their new home. Poltergeists are entities that haunt a specific place, not a family. The 30 East Drive tale tells of the home still being haunted to this very day, so why the short span of the Gill Lane haunting?

The current residents were happy for me to publish the story but asked not to have their house number divulged. They have lived in the property for just under two years without incident. The family before them owned the house for nearly fifteen years with not so much as a single drawer opening.

With the evidence as it is, it appears that the Gill Lane poltergeist may indeed have been nothing more than a hoax, committed by someone of flesh and blood. The only other solution is that the phenomena truly did happen, and the malevolent entity is simply lurking in the shadows, waiting for the time to strike.

West Street, Sheffield

The strange story of the phantom highwayman that haunts a popular public house in Sheffield, takes place on one of the more prominent streets in the city and becomes even more unusual due to the lifelike form of the manifestation. It is said to be so real that hundreds of people may have encountered it without even giving it a second thought, let alone considering the prospect that they may have just seen a ghost.

The Wick at Both Ends public house on West Street, formerly known as the Mail Coach after being an office of Royal Mail in the mid-nineteenth century, is the home to this particular phantom that is regularly spotted outside dressed in a black cape and hat.

The apparition hides around the corner of the building, watching and waiting for the perfect opportunity to commit robbery, before either vanishing right before bewildered spectators' eyes or proceeding to enter the doors of the pub.

Many have witnessed this phenomenon, assuming it to be one of the students at the nearby university playing a prank and therefore dismissing the incident only to think it strange when discussing with others who have also encountered the phantom highwayman.

One gentleman, thinking it was part of a show, followed the spirit through the entrance of the pub, only to be greeted by bewildered staff and customers with no knowledge of the manifestation that had just entered the building they occupied.

In the days when the Wick at Both Ends was a Royal Mail office, it would have been subjected to many robberies, and it was even believed to have been held up by the infamous John Nevison, the highwayman famed not only for his gentlemanly nature but also his amazing feat of speed to evade capture in 1676.

After committing a robbery in Kent, he rode an incredible 200 miles in a single day, on a single horse, before drinking with a magistrate in a pub in York that evening which led to him being acquitted of the crime. The magistrate testified that he'd been drinking with Nevison and no one believed he could possibly have committed a crime in Kent that morning and have been drinking in York that evening.

His fame spread quickly and he even gained the personal nickname of 'Swift Nick' from King Charles II himself. The Three Houses Inn at Wakefield proudly displays a plaque stating that Nevison was arrested there prior to his execution in York in 1685.

But is John Nevison really haunting the Wick at Both Ends on West Street in Sheffield? Or is another highwayman carrying out his dastardly deeds in the afterlife?

The area of West Street in Sheffield where the infamous phantom of the highwayman is regularly spotted.

It's interesting that the phantom is assumed to be the infamous John Nevison, as though the tale of a ghostly apparition lurking in the alleyways on West Street isn't worthy in its own right, and therefore needed to be of someone famous to give it that extra panache.

Perhaps, in a time when pubs are not getting the customers they used to, it's merely a publicity stunt or ongoing joke by someone of flesh and blood that, after being retold on so many occasions, has turned into a local folk tale.

Perhaps it's little more than a single tale from an imaginative mind that has taken on a life of its own as the story spreads. Or maybe an unworldly spirit truly does lurk in the alleyways of West Street, waiting for his perfect opportunity to strike again.

Ecclesall Woods

The beautiful Ecclesall Woods offer walking routes, a wide range of animals to spot, and a location laced with history, including the Second World War bomb crater that dates back to December of 1940. With all it has to offer, it's little wonder that the woodland has made a name for itself as a popular tourist attraction with visiting families and school trips alike. It's growing in popularity each and every year, but amid all the birds chirping, animals rustling and children playing, the woodland houses a dark secret: a tale not of witches or ghosts, but of the most heinous of all creatures, a demon.

As the local legend goes, deep in the heart of the woods, just south of the dry cavity that would have once been home to a swamp, lives a woodland demon, believed by some to be a Leshy. The folklore surrounding this mysterious beast is ambiguous at best: some claim it to be a friendly and approachable creature that can lure you away and tickle you to death, whilst others claim it can be used for pacts, much like a crossroads demon.

This particular demonic entity is commonly believed to be a wish granter, the devilish twist being that the Leshy can see a person's soul and therefore, grant the wish accordingly. There are numerous stories of its appearance, from that of a goat-like creature that can talk, to stories of a beautiful maiden who lures unsuspecting men to an early death, mirroring the Siren legend. Ecclesall Wood's folk tale has the Leshy appear in the form of a bearded old man.

It is believed to be a protective demon that allows the woodland to flourish and there are numerous stories surrounding this legend with different outcomes. After researching many of them, the two I've chosen to share with you showcase both aspects of the legend of the Leshy that resides in Ecclesall Woods.

A local man, who wished not to be named, told me of an almost unbelievable encounter with the beast back in 2009. He said he was walking in the woods one day with a view to killing himself. His wife had left him, he'd lost his job and he'd been evicted from his home.

With his entire life spiralling out of control, he simply wanted to end it all and found himself wandering the woodland, searching for a way to do it. As he neared the old swamp, he sat upon a fallen tree and, with tears streaming down his face, he recalls feeling 'at rock bottom'.

As the man sat upon a fallen tree trunk, an elderly gentleman wandered by and, seeing him in a clearly distressed state, asked if he was okay. The man nodded, wishing to be left alone, and the elderly man just smiled, placing a £1 coin on the tree trunk and telling the man his luck would turn before wandering off along the paths and into the trees.

After an hour or so, the man walked back out of the woods feeling worse than ever. He couldn't even kill himself properly. As he wandered down the road he passed a shop with a National Lottery Instants sign in the window. Feeling in his pocket, he remembered he'd picked up the coin the man had given him and made his way inside the shop to buy a scratch card. After scratching it off in the shop, he discovered he'd won £50,000.

The man went on to tell me he used the money to invest in a business he'd always dreamed of and now he is the proud owner of one of the largest manufacturing companies in Yorkshire.

Whilst this story has an air of fairytale about it, the fundamentals all check out when researched. The man did win £50,000 on a scratch card, he did buy equipment within six months of winning it and now he does own one of the biggest manufacturing companies in Yorkshire.

I don't doubt for a second that he wandered off into Ecclesall Woods that day and it's plausible that he bought the scratch card on his way home. The question is, did he really encounter the old man and if so, was he the infamous Leshy?

Another story that caught my eye was of a woman called Sarah Fisher. Sarah works in management for a company in Sheffield and is responsible for firing people, amongst other things. She told me that on the Friday prior to her tale, she'd had to fire a young man who was incompetent at his job, but it weighed heavily upon her as the chap had recently had a new baby and she worried about his financial position. Of course, the world of business is no place for sentiment but, as a human, she felt a sense of guilt in the build-up to her strange tale.

Whilst out walking her dog on the Sunday afternoon following the young man's dismissal, Sarah's little Jack Russell ran off through the trees as it chased a rabbit. Sarah spent a few minutes running in the direction that her pet had run, calling after the animal and whistling.

Soon after, she arrived at the old swamp, an area she claimed to have never stumbled upon before.

Sarah went on to tell me that an elderly gentleman was sitting on a rock, fishing in the shallow water that had collected with the recent downpour. The dirty green water clearly couldn't be home to any life, but there he was. She asked the man if he'd seen her dog and he told her to follow the easterly path, as that's where the dog had gone. She also recalls him muttering something about looking after the animal properly.

Sarah, ignoring the man's words, quickly ran down the thin winding path in search of her companion. After a few minutes, the path stopped abruptly as a large, old oak tree was growing straight over her route with no way of getting through.

Sarah called for her dog once again, and he came running from the bushes. Relieved to see him at last, she put on his lead and started to make her way back towards the old swamp when a branch from a tree fell, striking the dog on his head and killing him instantly. Sarah was distraught and picked up the animal to carry him home and, at that moment, she claims to have heard a loud sound echoing around the woods that sounded, for a second, almost like an old man laughing.

Neither of these storytellers ever saw the old man again, and remain unsure as to whether it was his doing that led to their strange tales. Sarah even claimed to have never heard the folk tale before, whilst the man openly admitted that he was familiar with the area and the Leshy legend.

These are two that I have picked out to share but there are upwards of ten similar accounts, all offering a happy or sad ending and most of which claim to have encountered an old man with a long beard.

Are these simply local folklore tales that have begun to spread? For me, I think it's correct to notice the subtle undertones of the stories. They all seem to share the characteristics found in the Brothers Grimm tales. Perhaps the Ecclesall Woods Leshy was simply made up by parents to stop their children venturing too far into the woodlands in times gone by.

The man's tale has an air of romance about it but it's hard to comprehend why Sarah would have made up such a brutal tale that clearly still saddened her to this day. It's also worth noting that she carries a picture of the Jack Russell in her purse, whether to remember her pet or use as a prop for the tale is down to your own personal opinion.

The legend itself offers little in the form of evidence: a Leshy is indeed a woodland spirit, but it is of Slavic origin and therefore wouldn't normally reside in the UK. It's also believed to be a wish granter, but to what end is its purpose to protect the woodland?

Perhaps it's a combination of different legends that have collided into the story it is now. Maybe the legend is true but it's a different creature altogether. On face value, it seems reasonable to put the stories down to fabricated tales from attention-seeking minds. Or maybe, just maybe, there is a demonic Leshy in Ecclesall Woods with powers beyond our own comprehension.

St Nicholas' Church, High Bradfield

We've all heard the tale of Burke and Hare, the infamous body snatchers that preferred to kill their victims rather than go through the rigmarole of digging up fresh corpses around Edinburgh in 1828.

Those prolific killers seem to have gained all the fame from that old profession, but in actual fact, the first cases of body snatching were reported in 1742, right here in South Yorkshire, eighty-six years before the infamous reign of the aforementioned despicable duo.

During that time, surgeons were in dire need of fresh cadavers for their continued anatomy research, but people were becoming more reluctant to donate their loved ones to the cause. The thought of having them cut open on a surgeon's table as opposed to resting in peace for eternity wasn't worth the coins they'd receive in exchange.

An organised crime group known as the Resurrectionists answered the doctors' calls and began digging up fresh corpses that could be sold to the surgeons for a good price, given the lack of available subjects.

One of their favourite places to target was the old resting place in the sleepy village of High Bradfield. At first, the gang worked unnoticed, but after a short while, people realised they were being targeted.

In a bid to protect their loved ones' eternal resting places, the residents built a watchtower in the graveyard that is still there to this day. After a loved one was laid to rest, a family member or friend would inhabit the tower, ensuring the lamp could be seen clearly from the top window to ward off any potential thieves. They would remain at their post for a week or so, after which the rotting corpses would no longer be acceptable to the surgeons and therefore, not worth digging up.

It's unclear how many corpses were removed from this graveyard, as people were naturally reluctant to exhume their own dead family members to check that they were, in fact, still buried. The figure is thought to be a higher number than in most areas at the time though, as the remote village situated on a high point of South Yorkshire was the perfect location for the thieves to work undetected.

Body snatching ceased around 1832, following the infamous trial of Burke and Hare that brought the horrific money-making racket into the public eye and gave cause for the Anatomy Act to be passed, tightening the regulations upon doctors and surgeons.

St Nicholas' Church has been rife with tales of spooky goings-on ever since. Shadowy figures of the undead, light anomalies around certain graves and eerie groans echoing around the night sky are just a few of the things you might encounter.

Being a religious place, it would be in bad taste to ghost hunt on the premises, however I did find a local paranormal group that was able to stop in the watchtower overnight to investigate the phenomena in 2012. Matthew Frost, one of the lead investigators, met with me to share their story:

> It was a Friday night and we set up in the watchtower with cameras covering the graveyard and suspected graves of interest.

The night was quite disappointing at first: from six in the evening until nearly four in the morning, not a single thing occurred.

Then, out of nowhere, strange groans were heard floating around the churchyard. We dashed to the window to look and there we saw what appeared to be flickering shadows, wandering between the graves. The noise was really strange, more like something you'd expect to hear in a cheap zombie movie than real life.

I remember it also went really cold. I know it was winter, but I mean really cold. You could literally feel the temperature drop but our digital thermometers didn't change at all. We watched on as the shadowy beings walked the churchyard, and filmed them with a handheld camera, as well as the camera that was set up all night in the top window of the watchtower.

The really bizarre and quite disappointing thing happened when we checked our footage the following day. There were no shadows, no light anomalies and unfortunately, no groaning sounds.

The old church in High Bradfield with the watchtower to the rear, just before the houses.

You can hear us react to the phenomena, see the cameras looking over the points of interest and hear us discussing the events unfolding before our eyes, but not a single thing was captured on film.

I'm positive that we saw the restless spirits of High Bradfield burial ground that night, but I guess they didn't really want to be seen. I suppose that's the strange thing about the paranormal.

I looked over Matthew's video footage and it does seem to be genuine. They all react to the sounds and images described with what appears to be genuine fear, which would be hard to fabricate.

Of course, we must remember that, by his own admission, the team had been sitting in a graveyard in the middle of winter for ten hours and, therefore, it would not be unreasonable to assume both the cold and boredom may have played their part in this account.

The remote location is home to various animals and birds and it's possible that they heard one of these. As the group were eager to experience some kind of phenomena, pareidolia may have simply caused them to imagine the things they claim to have encountered.

Of course, that's just a rational mind thinking. You may equally question, are the restless spirits of those removed from the High Bradfield burial ground still wandering the area at night? Desperately trying to escape the purgatory that they reside in so that they can finally rest in peace?

School Hill, Whiston

The beautiful church of St Magdalene, located at the very peak of the picturesque School Hill, in Whiston in Rotherham, is an eerily beautiful church that looks as though it would lay claim to numerous ghostly stories. It is, however, the walk up to the church that would most likely provide a strange and unusual encounter.

From a historical point of view, the reason for the ghostly sightings is as confusing as they are scary. The area has never been the home to a great tragedy involving the deaths of children, nor was it the location of the bubonic plague, thanks to the heroic actions of the villagers of Eyam in the seventeenth century.

Despite these factors, numerous sightings of a group of children, often described as being dressed in old-fashioned clothes, have been reported within the fields by many different people.

The children are said to appear, holding hands and singing 'Ring-a-Ring-o'-Roses' in an eerily spooky song, before vanishing into thin air. They have been spotted by no fewer than twenty people and there are likely to be many more who haven't retold their strange accounts on School Hill.

The most confusing part of the tale derives from the song that the childish spectres are reported to be singing. 'Ring-a-Ring-o'-Roses' was a common song during the bubonic plague and told of the misconception that the smell of rose petals would protect people from catching the pestilence.

It's worth noting that in nearby Herringthorpe, there is a mass grave for those who died of cholera in the late nineteenth century, 200 years after the plague hit the Derbyshire town of Eyam, although my research has shown that many people believe the cholera site to actually be a plague burial ground. Could it be that the history between the two is becoming distorted as time passes by?

Alan Baines was visiting the church one day for a christening when he wandered up the hill, having parked at its foot. This is Alan's story:

> It was mid-November and a beautiful sunny day. It was still early, and the frost was glistening on the field next to me. I remember admiring the landscape as I walked up the hill and towards the church. You can just see the M1 motorway in the distance, which I remember thinking spoilt the timeless scene somewhat.
>
> As I neared the top, I looked at the horses and then, from nowhere, a group of kids appeared behind them. They were all

holding hands and singing but at first, I wasn't sure what the song was. It was only when they fell to the ground I realised it was 'A Ring of Roses.'

I remember thinking it was somewhat strange to see them playing so close to the clearly spooked horses, but they seemed unaware of their presence. As they hit the floor, one of the stallions crossed in front of my view but, as it moved away, the children were all gone.

It didn't even cross my mind that they might have been ghostly apparitions until I was discussing it with friends after, at the christening. They were from the Whiston area and told me of the folklore surrounding School Hill.

I hear that animals are more in tune with the spirit world than humans, so I suppose that might well have been what spooked the horses, yet they seemed perfectly happy to walk towards anyone wandering up the hill. To this day I can't be sure, but it's certainly a strange one.

The notorious field next to School Hill in Whiston where the childish spectres have been regularly spotted.

According to Alan, the ghostly children did not appear in such a way that he immediately thought they were unearthly, as many others who have claimed to have seen them. They were so solid, in fact, that he just assumed that they were normal children, playing in the field.

The only thing to be certain of is that there are no manholes, no secret bunkers or dips and no way of disappearing from view without being seen to run away. But if the spectres truly are spirits, why that song?

Were they perhaps plague victims that were unaccounted for? Could they have been cholera victims that simply liked the childhood song? Or maybe they are just the product of imagination, existing only in imaginative minds.

Hangman Stone Lane, Marr

This rural stretch of lane in Marr is the home of a strange tale that has been the focal point of numerous paranormal investigations ever since. According to local folklore, Johnathon Holt was a young man who preferred stealing for a living rather than a hard day's work. It was that desire for easy money that inevitably ended his life prematurely in a brutal, if not slightly comical, way back in the mid-nineteenth century.

As the story goes, Johnathon had been out one evening along that rural stretch of the lane, when he saw the opportunity to steal a large ram from the fields adjacent. We can assume he stole the animal to sell it as he chose not to kill it on site but instead, bound its legs together and proceeded to carry it over his shoulders. Evidently, walking the animal home would have been too easy for this thief.

When he arrived at the large stone, which was at one time reportedly used as a gallows, he stopped to rest, placing the ram on top of it safe in the knowledge it would be unable to escape.

The frightened animal lost its footing and slipped, leaving it dangling in mid-air halfway down the rear side of the stone.

Sadly for Johnathon, the rope that bound the animal's feet had got caught around his neck, strangling him to death as the constriction tightened.

The next morning, a man travelling towards Marr spotted the animal dangling upside down on the stone and approached to investigate the bizarre sight in front of him. Upon examination, he also discovered the lifeless body of Johnathon, his head bulging and blue as the makeshift noose constricted the flow of blood.

Ironically, the ram was in fact still alive, albeit barely, having spent the entire evening upside down. As local police attended the scene, the animal was returned back to its rightful owner where it was nursed back to full health whilst the body of Johnathon Holt was cut down and tossed in an unmarked grave by the hangman's stone. He was a known thief with a kidnapped ram so there was no point in pursuing the usual rigmarole of investigating his death.

Ever since that strange night, there have been numerous sightings of a phantom man by the stone that seemingly vanishes into thin air before the eyes of unsuspecting drivers. There have even been reports of motorists stopping to help a young man, believing him to have been injured, only to find he'd disappeared and just a disembodied gurgling sound remained, haunting the night sky.

Dave Price was driving along Hangman Stone Lane on a misty night in 2013 when he experienced this strange apparition:

I was on my way home from work and passing the area like I did five nights a week. I saw a kid, slumped by the side of the road. I pulled up the car to see if he was okay and as I got out of my car, I heard the strange whimpering sound he was making.

I thought 'bloody hell, this kid's really hurt here,' so I rushed over to help him, but as soon as I got close, he'd vanished into thin air. Nowhere to be seen.

I thought he'd run away but it was only a few weeks after, when someone in the pub was talking about the ghost story, I thought, 'Hang on, I might have actually seen something there.'

Dave's story is an interesting account and he's the very stereotype of a no-nonsense Yorkshireman, and therefore credible to a certain degree. Even as he spoke, I could tell he didn't really believe the strange story coming out of his own mouth, almost as though he was questioning it the entire time.

Although this legend has no evidence to support it and the reality is, the story makes little sense, the sightings do pose the question, did the thief really die in this way and his tainted soul stain the fabric of time, allowing people still to encounter the echo to this day?

Or is it just a charming folk tale that was told by the locals in times gone by to warn children against stealing other people's property?

Loxley Common, Loxley

Loxley Common, situated close to Hillsborough Golf Club, is the setting for a local folklore legend that features a woman in white, commonly believed to be the restless spirit of Mary Revill who was brutally bludgeoned to death in the early twentieth century.

Mary, a spinster, was the wife of gamekeeper William and mother of their baby boy Henry. On the night prior to her death, she had been looking after the child whilst her husband was in his cabin at the far side of the woods.

On New Year's Day, a gentleman from a neighbouring hamlet was passing through Loxley Common, which was covered in fresh snow, when he spotted footsteps accompanied by a trail of what appeared to be blood, splattered over the white landscape.

The trail was coming from the door of Revill's cottage and headed off into the woodland, so the concerned gentleman rapped the door of the cottage, but nobody answered. Noticing the door was unlocked, the man entered the property and to his shock, found the lifeless body of Mary lying face down on the

The infamous cave in Loxley Common remains cordoned off to the public to this day.

floor, her baby sleeping soundly in his cot just a few feet from his late mother.

Reporting the incident immediately to the nearby police station at Hillsborough, which has since been demolished, a search party headed out into the woods. The officers and dogs followed the bloody trail that eventually led to a cave, deep within Loxley Common. As there was only a single trail of footsteps, the search party assumed the perpetrator was still within the dark cavity, so they proceeded to enter with caution.

A thorough search of both the cave and the nearby area provided no evidence or clues, and with no enemies or suspects that would have wished harm upon Mary, suspicion quickly fell upon her husband, the eccentric drunkard William Revill.

He had been seen drinking in the local tavern on the night before the murder and was described as heavily intoxicated. Police discovered William sleeping off the ale in his cabin. There were no footsteps, no blood and no other trails leading in or out. It was clear he'd been alone for the entirety of the night and as such, no charges were made.

Following the incident, the cave was avoided by the locals who believed it to be an evil place. William continued to work as the gamekeeper, but his drinking became heavier and he visibly aged. His hair and beard turned as white as the snow at only 42 years old. He spiralled into a deep depression following the death of his wife, and the baby boy was naturally taken away by the authorities.

A year or so after the murder, locals commented on not having seen William for a good few days, so a small group of friends went out into Loxley Common towards his cabin, to check up on the man. Upon arrival, all seemed quiet but, after entering the cabin, they found William's corpse hanging from the beams that ran along the ceiling.

A search of the cabin uncovered a rusty old knife and a pair of his trousers that were covered in blood. Had the police made a terrible mistake by not charging the man? Or were the trousers simply bloody on account of hunting within the common?

To this day there are reports of a woman's voice singing delicate lullabies to her baby boy, which echo eerily around the common during the winter months. In addition, the apparition of a white woman floating through the trees and around the cave entrance has also become a regular sighting in the area. More disturbingly, strange noises are also reported to come from within the cave, often compared to the sound of a lunatic laughing.

The tale is well known around the area but is often retold with numerous variations, as you'd expect with any folklore legend. Some claim it was a woman that found Mary; others say the cave was directly underneath the house. The fundamentals never change though: the single trail of footsteps leading into the cave, William being found in his cabin and the baby boy sleeping soundly through the brutal killing of his mother.

It does make one wonder, if William truly did murder his wife, why were the footprints heading into the cave but never back out? Why was he found over a mile away in his cabin? Why was her body still within their home?

Was William truly the murderer? Or had Mary fallen foul of another being beyond our mortal realm? Of course, the biggest question is, do the spirits of Mary and William still haunt Loxley Common to this day?

Low Valley Arms, Wombwell

The Low Valley Arms public house in Wombwell was the setting for a bizarre tale that occurred in 2006 and has become something of a local legend around Wombwell after being documented within local newspapers at the time. One thing that really makes the tale stand out is the fact that it was not only witnessed by the landlord, but also police officers adding an air of credibility to this terrifying account of alleged paranormal activity.

As the story goes, on a mild April evening of that year, the then current landlord and his wife retired to bed having locked up and secured the building as usual. He was described as being a large, no-nonsense man, the very stereotype of a rural pub landlord and his wife was similar in build and personality.

On that particular evening, the couple were awoken around 1 a.m. by the sound of someone rummaging around in the pub downstairs. Believing they were being burgled, the landlord grabbed the bat that he kept positioned by his bed before running downstairs, shouting loudly and stomping his feet in a bid to frighten away the perpetrators without confrontation.

When he arrived downstairs, closely followed by his fearless wife, they noticed that all the televisions were turned on and the room was illuminated also by the light of the jukebox. The couple stated that even though there wasn't any music playing, they were certain that they had turned off all the appliances the previous night, as they did every evening.

At this point, the landlord believed that they had indeed been burgled and figured the items had been switched on in some kind of macabre practical joke by the thieves. As his wife turned off the televisions and the jukebox, he went off to search the building, checking both the safe and the tills, all of which had been loaded with a £50 float for the following day.

Realising that nothing had been taken, his bewildered wife called the police to report the incident and officers were sent to the premises immediately. Whilst they were en route, the landlord continued to check the pub for any signs of damage or clues. After checking the gentlemen's toilets, which seemed to be untouched, he went to check the ladies.

His wife stated that she watched him walk inside the restroom before running out a few seconds later with a look of sheer panic on his face. He then proceeded to tell her of the gruesome sight that he had encountered, describing a naked woman of flesh and bone, dripping in blood and with half her jaw missing, slumped in one of the cubicles.

The frightened couple wondered if the woman had been assaulted and, at the request of his wife, the landlord returned into the toilet to offer any assistance until the police arrived. Once back inside, however, there was no sign of the woman or of any of the blood he'd claimed to have seen previously.

Shortly after, the police arrived and listened to the tale from the clearly shaken-up publican and his wife. As the landlord was telling his version of the events to the officers, a toilet was heard to flush in the ladies. The officers and the landlord quickly returned to the restroom to investigate.

Whilst inside the toilets, they all claimed to have witnessed the three cubicles start to flush, over and over by an unseen hand. Not only was it peculiar that there wasn't anyone flushing them, they could offer no explanation for where the water was coming from as the cisterns would have been unable to refill as the toilets violently flushed continuously for a good few minutes.

Spooked by the strange goings-on, the officers fled, closely followed by the landlord and his wife, escaping through the bar area towards the door. As they rushed through, all of the televisions turned on for a second time right in front of their eyes.

That night the landlord and his wife stayed with friends and never returned to their pub after those strange happenings in 2006. The pub closed permanently soon after and has now been converted for other use.

One really interesting point worth mentioning is that this was by all accounts an isolated incident. Unlike other tales of haunted pubs, there were no previous accounts of paranormal phenomena. No children laughing, ghostly footsteps, deceased landlords of times gone by, shadows lurking in the cellar or glasses and ashtrays being thrown across the room. Does this add credibility to the account? Or perhaps, make it more likely to have been an isolated hoax?

The fact that the landlord felt the need to keep a weapon by his bed suggests that, at the time, this may have been an unsavoury area and therefore it could have been a burglary gone wrong, the thieves fleeing as the sound of the landlord bellowed around the pub.

The toilets may have been acting strangely due to bad plumbing and the appliances could have been accidentally left on from the previous evening. The strange woman may have been the product of an overactive mind as his broken sleep and the looming threat of trespassers caused his imagination to play tricks. Remember, of all the people there that evening, he was the only one that saw the gruesome apparition.

Could this have been the product of tricksters or perhaps an angry customer? Or was there something more sinister lurking in the Low Valley Arms on that strange April night in 2006? Perhaps it was the restless spirit of a woman, injured in times gone by, who still resides with the building?

Nabs Wood, Silkstone Common

At the home of one of the worst disasters that England has ever seen, dozens of ghostly children are said to haunt the eerie woodlands and they have been spotted more so than any other allegedly haunted area I have encountered.

With a combination of such sadness and intrigue, it seems only fitting that our journey across South Yorkshire should end here at Nabs Wood where ghostly laughter is commonly heard around the area as the imp-like spectres are regularly spotted, hiding behind trees in what appears to be a spectral game of hide and seek.

The story as to why the area is haunted dates back to 1838 when heavy rain poured into the mine below. On 4 July of that year, a stiflingly hot afternoon caused the build-up of humidity to explode in the most violent of ways. Hailstone and torrential rain fell upon Silkstone for more than two hours, causing flash flooding all over the area.

During the downpour, many young children were working down in Huskar Pit as they would have done for generations, the youngest of whom worked as designated trappers, ensuring the air doors were shut tight as the older children, working as hurriers, passed by with the coal that they relayed from the mine to the pit shaft.

Given the high price of candles, these children would usually work in complete darkness, feeling their way around the mineshafts using their hands. Often, they would be working for up to fourteen hours a day in a bid to bring a few extra pence to the meagre family table.

On that fateful day, as the thunder bellowed from the sky above the pit, the water headed towards the mine, extinguishing the fire that powered the steam engine responsible for powering the lift that was used to raise the workers and coal from the deep shafts below.

As the rainwater poured in, the children became frightened and scrambled for safety. They would have been undoubtedly terrified and weak, having already been in the mine for over nine hours that day.

In a bid to escape, the young workers joined a small drift that was heading out towards Nabs Wood. Many other children chose to use this method and joined them as they made their way along the water to safety, but it was a move that sealed their fates.

The memorial stone and sculpture in Silkstone Common, commemorating the lives tragically lost in 1838.

As dozens of the mites paddled along the drift, a stream that had burst its bank high above the mine poured in, turning their exit path into a raging torrent and inevitably drowning all but six of the young children, thrashing their lifeless bodies out into the woodland.

One 10-year-old boy named George Burkinshaw was discovered clutching the body of his younger brother James who was only 7, as the pair drowned together on that fateful day.

As miners, locals and the authorities sieved through the piles of fallen trees, rocks and small bodies, the severity of the tragedy became clear – so much so in fact, that Queen Victoria herself intervened and started the enquiry into children and women working in the mines. Despite the outrage from the mine owners who wanted to capitalise on the cheap labour that the children offered, in 1842 the government passed a

A separate memorial in pride of place at Silkstone church, around 1 mile away from the Huskar pit site.

new Mines Act, forbidding any such employer to use women or children in their workforce.

There are monuments and plaques around Nabs Wood and Silkstone Common that commemorate the young children that lost their lives in such a sad way all those years ago, and one would wonder if these tributes, combined with the indisputable sadness associated with the area, are enough to force the mind to imagine the ghostly stories that are told here.

Numerous local paranormal groups have visited this place over the years and, in addition to capturing numerous light anomalies on camera, they have also filmed footage of Ouija board sessions that correctly identify the names, ages and dates of many of the children that lost their lives that day.

The issue with this is that the names and ages of the victims are written on many of the tributes, and therefore it's perfectly reasonable to assume they already knew the answers to the questions that they were asking, prior to the session starting.

The area itself certainly has a macabre feel to it and it's little wonder that people might think they experience some kind of paranormal phenomena here. That, of course, is not to say the phenomena aren't true. There have been numerous sightings of the children, from ordinary day-to-day dog walkers and ramblers, to families enjoying a picnic and out-of-towners driving past the woodland and entrance to the common.

Whether they truly still haunt the area or not is a matter of belief, but for me, the main question is, are these people smearing the legacies of the children that lost their lives in such a horrific way, simply to progress with their own careers?

Am I disrespecting their memories by retelling this tale? Or are the ghostly imps really playing in the woods in the afterlife, happy and safe at last? I for one, hope they are.

3

Ghosts

Paranormal investigators, parapsychologists and thrill seekers alike enjoy visiting alleged haunted places in search of ghosts, but what actually is a ghost? A form of unexplained energy, a memory, a legacy, or a person's soul that is unable to leave our mortal realm after death?

Traditionally a ghost, also known as an apparition, spectre, phantom or spirit, is believed to be the energy of a soul that has passed. Sometimes that energy is strong enough to manifest as a full-bodied apparition that can be seen as an actual figure. Other times it is thought to be a source of energy that cannot be explained by science, an anomaly of electromagnetic field (EMF) or sudden drops in temperature with no apparent reason.

Psychics claim to be in tune with this energy and from it, they can pick up on names and dates associated with the person whose energy they claim to be seeing or feeling, but are they truly picking up on the things they claim to receive?

Orbs are strange light anomalies that were originally believed to be seen only on night vision cameras, but these days people claim to see them on any digital device and even with the naked eye. They are thought to be the first manifestation of a ghost but, despite being captured on numerous pieces of footage, they never develop into an actual spirit on film. Certain orbs or light anomalies are of particular interest from a scientific point of view. These are the orbs that appear with a clear nucleus in the centre, the heartbeat from where the light is formed if you will.

Any orb without a nucleus is most probably nothing more than dust, an insect or a light flare, despite their unusual appearance when first spotted. The fact that people will only see what they want to see can give these everyday light anomalies a different meaning, leaving them open to interpretation as with almost all evidence of the afterlife.

Poltergeist activity is thought to be that of a spirit that cannot be seen but has the ability to move objects or touch people. It is likely that this theory has adapted over time as traditionally, a poltergeist wasn't a ghost or spirit at all. It was a malevolent entity somewhere between spirits and demons. Unlike other spirits that are said to manifest, a poltergeist can never be seen and instead, hides under the cover of invisibility and uses its abilities to throw or move objects for the living to see.

The ghosts that intrigue me the most are known as echoes: the woman in white staring from the window of a stately home or the grey lady wandering the stalls of an old theatre. With so much emotion involved throughout their lives, these sightings are believed to be marks on the fabric of time that can be seen over and over without interaction or knowledge of being watched. I believe, of all the theories, these are the most plausible as their highly emotional state during life could have effectively stained time.

There are also the stories of ghosts in visitation. These spectres are not tied to a specific location but are free to come and go as they please, often returning from the afterlife to visit loved ones or watch over family members in times of grief or stress.

People claim to experience these apparitions daily, either by seeing the phantom as a full-bodied apparition or by experiencing strange phenomena that they believe to be a sign of their presence, usually things like taps turning on by an unseen hand or a light bulb flickering repeatedly for no known reason, but from a scientific point of view, it's possible that they are experiencing pareidolia, the term given for finding patterns in random events.

Some claim that ghosts can be harmful to humans; these are known as vengeful spirits. The folklore surrounding these dangerous phantoms suggests that they chose not to leave our mortal realm for various reasons, often tied in again with their own personal emotions in life. The pain of leaving a loved one, the fear of what could be waiting for them in the afterlife, or the inability to separate themselves from the emotions they felt on earth are all common causes of these types of ghosts.

As time passes by, whatever they remained on earth to be with would, eventually, pass over or change. These spirits are then left with nothing but bitterness and hatred, which they turn on the humans they have become envious of for still being alive.

One interesting point worth mentioning is that paranormal investigators always claim to send these spirits 'into the light'. Of course, this is a religious theory, the light symbolising heaven or the afterlife. This intrigues me because the actual bible states that humans should be servants of God in order to enter the kingdom of heaven.:

> Now the works of the flesh are evident: sexual immorality, impurity, sensuality, idolatry, sorcery, enmity, strife, jealousy, fits of anger, rivalry, envy, drunkenness, orgies, and things like these. I warn you, as I have warned you before, that those who do such things will not inherit the kingdom of God.
>
> (Galatians 5:19-21)

As the afterlife is tied in with the theories of heaven and hell, I find the idea of trying to send these lost spirits to the light rather strange, as who can truly enter the light with such a strict code of conduct? In addition, if they are not being sent into the light, where are they being sent?

Considering every aspect, it is little wonder that people claim to experience all kinds of phenomena, as the comfort it offers is much needed in times of strife. Of course, the experiences of taps turned on and such like are somewhat contradicted by the belief that poltergeists are the only entities that can actually interact with people and objects but, as with everything paranormal, ghosts are a matter of belief, not fact.

The afterlife will remain a mystery until our own time arrives, so whether it is real paranormal phenomena or simply pareidolia, people take from these experiences what they can and in doing so, comfort themselves and keep a legacy alive. To me, that's what is magical about the subject: the legacies that live on through the tales.

4

Psychic Controversy

Around the world, there are certain individuals who claim to possess psychic powers: the ability to see, feel and hear the energy of those who have passed over to the other side or connect with certain objects that they claim still holds the energies of the past.

This phenomenon fascinates me and, whenever possible, I love nothing more than studying these people in the hope of meeting someone who can demonstrate genuine psychic abilities that will astound me.

The whole world of psychics is very ambiguous and, from a scientific point of view, those claiming to have psychic abilities are most likely charlatans, unscrupulous individuals who earn a living trampling upon the memory of the deceased. But then why is there a billion-pound industry built around the topic if it is fake?

Over the past ten years, I have analysed thousands of clairvoyants in my own attempts to figure out the truth. The vast majority I have to say used techniques that are commonly used by fraudulent mediums, namely cold reading and Barnum statements.

Cold reading is the ability to make yourself sound as though you are in touch with very personal information about the sitter, when in fact you are simply telling them facts that would most likely fit and then allowing them to join the dots for you.

Barnum statements, named for the showman PT Barnum (who recently came back into the public eye due to the hit movie *The Greatest Showman)*, a man who supposedly said 'there's something for everyone', a phrase he used when referring to psychics and other fortune-telling acts.

Barnum quickly realised that there are ways of asking questions that open them up for any answer. They can also be statements that feel very personal but apply to almost everyone, like horoscopes for instance.

A good example of cold reading would be stating that the alleged spirit of an elderly man or woman had chest pains. There's nothing unusual about this at all. Heart attacks are still one of the most common causes of death and failing a heart attack, most elderly people find themselves short of breath and such like in their twilight years.

Another common scenario would be when the psychic states that they're in contact with a lady (or man) and that they are sensing that they are a sister or mother type figure (or father, or brother). Again, these are very generalised statements and usually, those people visiting psychics are looking to hear from someone in particular and therefore will nod or make some other subconscious movement or gesture that tells the psychic the sitter can relate.

After an initial cold reading session, the psychic would then move onto Barnum statements. These can be observations such as: 'you go out with friends and you're lively and fun and the centre of attention – yet, when you get back home, you find yourself going over each word of every conversation and wondering what you might have said differently'.

Effectively they are just saying that the persona you put on in public is different from the deeply personal side which few see. This is human nature and something that everyone does, but if you already think that it's your father or grandfather saying these things, then you feel touched and happy and see the remarks as proof of the charlatan's abilities.

Another key thing to look out for would be the double negative: psychics will often add an extra word allowing them to react to both positive and negative answers. This, for example, could be something along the lines of, 'you've not been feeling unwell lately, have you?'

By adding the 'not' they can respond based on the sitter's answers. If they said they hadn't been well, the psychic would tell them that they should see their doctor. If they said they felt great, the psychic could follow with 'that's right, the spirits are telling me you're in great health.'

I always find it fascinating how in one breath, a medium will state there's a room full of spirits and they are all talking at once, yet as soon as it comes to direct chat, they can only offer a name or initial. I was at a performance recently and the psychic said he was joined by a man in a 1950s–styled suit. He then said that the spirit gave him the name Darren or Dave. Ask yourself, if you were a spirit visiting a loved one, what would you do? I'd say something along the lines of, 'there's our Chelsea, second row, fourth from the end, wearing a red jumper.'

I find it incredible that psychics expect us to believe that a spirit cannot even remember their own name. In actual fact, a sitter will say their father or grandfather was called Darren and before you know it, the name of Dave has been completely forgotten. Perhaps the spirits are simply unable to communicate clearly?

One very interesting fact worth noting is that the James Randi Educational Foundation in America offered $1 million to anyone who could demonstrate genuine psychic ability under test conditions. The experiment started in the 1960s lasted for over thirty years with not a single person collecting the prize, despite many attempts. Usually, the answer to this is that they didn't do it for money. Obviously, they must have forgotten to tell Sandra, who just paid £30 to speak with her dead cats.

During the production of this book, I made an offer to over ten people claiming to have psychic abilities: demonstrate for me, let me study you and enjoy your skills and, in turn, I will help promote you within my own set of connections. Every single one of them declined the offer.

During my mentalist days, I used to perform a great mind-reading trick (with the help of a friend). Between us, we named suits on a pack of cards. Hearts were Harry, diamonds were Dave, clubs were Chris and spades were Steve. Then counting ace through king, the thirteen numbers would correspond to a letter. Ace would be A, Deuce was a B, three was C and so on.

I'd then have a stranger pick a card at random and tell them that they could mentally tell another person which card it was without actually saying it. They'd pick the eight of diamonds for instance, so I'd put in the number of my friend and ask them to call Dave Harrison. Dave was diamonds and Harrison began with the eighth letter of the alphabet.

By asking for the name, my friend already knew which card had been picked, but by adding the showmanship of asking the spectator to really visualise the card, they would go away believing they had experienced genuine psychic ability. For me, that's what it all comes down to: suggestibility and showmanship.

In conclusion, it would be wrong of me to state that I didn't believe in any kind of psychic ability or phenomena. I wouldn't continue researching potential psychics if I did not. With that being said, I have never yet met one that I can honestly say I believed to have demonstrated genuine psychic abilities.

Maybe one day I'll be able to say otherwise but, in the meantime, enjoy the shows, don't take them too literally or personally and understand that, like any other show or performance, they are designed to entertain, so have fun.

But be wary of those crossing the line, and above all else, don't let psychics transform you from intelligent individuals into people who believe everything without question. If it doesn't make any sense, it's probably just not true. Your future has not yet been written; it's up to you to choose your own path in life.

5

The Various Colours of Ladies

Many ghost stories feature a lady of a specific colour who is said to haunt a certain area or place. The folklore surrounding these mysterious spirits states the colours are reflective of either the emotion felt within their mortal lives or the way in which they died, often through some kind of betrayal.

Generally speaking, there are five primary variations which are white, green, purple, grey and red, although often localised ghost stories will claim to have many other colours including blue, brown and pink.

Whilst it would be impossible for anyone to disprove these added variations, they are most commonly believed to actually be one of the main colours that either has insufficient energy to manifest fully or has become distorted through time. Another theory suggests that they show lesser traits of the main variations, an example being the dangerous purple lady. If she was to be less powerful she might appear as a blue lady.

Additionally, there is also the infamous black lady or woman in black. These entities are different from the shadows of the coloured ladies and by far the most dangerous of all.

White Lady

Commonly believed to be the lost spirit of a lady who experienced great tragedy in her life, usually the loss of a child or husband. Generally speaking, she would have died rather young and is often reported to be as beautiful in spirit as her soul was pure.

Her emotional state of loss and depression has made it impossible for this spirit to cross over. The white symbolises her purity, and it is believed that the white lady would have been faithful throughout her entire life and as such is lost in eternity, looking for her family or loved ones.

Green Lady

Derived from death involving water or woodlands, often having been murdered before having their corpse dumped for long enough that their soul has become one with the earth.

The green ladies are strong-willed and focused entities that look to punish all men, as they hold the gender responsible for taking their lives. The legend of the siren that sings a haunting song in the Scottish Highlands to lure men to an early grave is widely believed to be a very powerful variation of a green lady.

Purple Lady

A lady who was highly religious in life and often from a teaching background. These entities are rare but arguably the most dangerous of all the ladies, with the exception of the elusive woman in black.

Legend has it that a purple lady can see a person's soul and, much like the folklore surrounding angels, she is set on rewarding the just and punishing the wicked. She would have been very strict in life and with the kind of persona that was highly regarded as important within the community, but equally disliked by other mothers and children due to her ruthless ways.

It is said that if you come into contact with a purple lady, you must recite the Lord's Prayer in order for her to leave you unharmed.

Grey Lady

Very similar to the white lady, the grey lady is in fact thought by many to just be a noble version. Most grey ladies have spent large amounts of time feeling lost and pining for someone such as a lover lost at sea or a deceased child.

Many grey lady sightings are reported in old stately homes and they are believed to have been noble women who can still be seen, often staring out of a window, waiting for that someone to return.

These entities are oblivious to the changing world around them and can neither see nor hear anyone that tries to interact with them.

Lady in Red

Hell hath no fury like a woman scorned. The lady in red is believed to be the spirit of a prostitute that worked in or around the area where her spirit is spotted. Unlike the other ladies, this spirit gets her name from the red or scarlet dress that she wears in the afterlife, not from the overall colour of her astral appearance.

The lady in red is a strong and powerful entity, most likely due to the powerful character she possessed in order to survive life in the world's oldest profession. Unlike her counterparts, this spirit can appear as solid as you or I, and often people claim to have chatted with her before she unveils her true identity.

Her mortal work was thought to have been a way of keeping a lover in money before he left her with nothing, leaving her with bitterness and hatred for all men.

Mirroring the siren, it is believed that the lady in red (or red lady) will trick a male into bed before drinking their soul during sexual intercourse and killing them.

Another variation of this entity appears as a pink lady, although folklore states that she is not yet as powerful as her fully developed counterpart.

Black Lady

In addition to the aforementioned apparitions, it would not be right to forget the final spectral woman: one often forgotten due to the fact she is so rare and usually mistaken for a demon, or a male entity.

The black lady or woman in black is a soulless spirit who is not named amongst the five colours due to her overwhelming power. The black lady often appears as a dark shadow and her eternal colour is symbolic of her tainted soul.

Often, these malevolent entities will have murdered a husband, a child or a close friend, and the reason for them doing so was simply a case of hatred.

It is believed that in life, these entities were selfish and cruel individuals without any respect for the lives of others, and in death their dark souls have become even more powerful.

6

Pareidolia

Pareidolia is a psychological phenomenon that causes a rational mind to find patterns in random events and is something that we all experience in our day-to-day lives. As human beings, our brains are programmed to make sense of the world around us and everything that we see, touch, taste and hear.

Of course, there are times when random events occur with no rational explanation, and it is those things that cause us to experience pareidolia. The pictures we see in clouds, the face in the moon or devils dancing in flames are all classic examples of the phenomenon.

Whilst it is perfectly harmless, it can cause an issue when transferred into a paranormal setting. An example of this is an experiment that I have conducted numerous times over the years when we take a group of subjects and place them in an old house during the day and simply ask them to write down any noises that the house makes.

They will usually list things such as the electric buzzing and pipes knocking, or perhaps some external noises that have made their way in from outside amongst other various noises from within the building, such as a fridge whirring or a clock ticking. There's nothing unusual about these sounds, of course; everything makes a noise of some sort and it's virtually impossible to recreate a perfect silence.

This seemingly ghost-like apparition was found, upon closer inspection, to be little more than a natural ice sculpture as the water collected from the icicles above.

If we then took another group of subjects and placed them in the same building during the night and, after adding the extra suggestion that it was a haunted house, asked them to repeat the experiment, what would they write down?

Every buzz, knock and bang becomes proof of paranormal phenomena, but of course, we know that it's simply the same

A simple tree that has grown in such a way that it appears to have human characteristics.

sounds from the daytime, only the subjects are now experiencing heightened senses due to the suggestion that the building is haunted. This added element enables their minds to find patterns in the random events: pareidolia.

The biggest question to ask yourself is, would the places you've read about be as scary in the day without the aid of darkness to add an air of mystery to the location?

We will all have our own opinions, and nobody can truly give the answers, but pareidolia remains an interesting phenomenon and my research has found it to be responsible for the vast majority of alleged hauntings.

For the context of this book, are the ghostly pigs squealing in Settle simply animals from a neighbouring farm? Were the Busby Stoop deaths merely the product of alcohol consumption? Were the light anomalies at Upper Bradfield nothing more than insects and dust from the rural location? Were the toilets in the Low Valley Arms simply flushing due to bad plumbing?

Every paranormal encounter has an air of pareidolia to it and one must think carefully about the subject before drawing a conclusion. It is only by ruling out the rational that the irrational can be truly considered.

What appear to be orbs manifesting in Ecclesall Woods at night. Closer inspection proved them to be little more than a combination of insects, dust and other debris from the trees.

7

Black Dogs

For as long as man has been able to tell stories, there have been tales of strange spectral dogs that are often associated with death or the devil. These mysterious beasts are said to be much larger than a regular dog and have been described generally as abnormally large Irish wolfhounds or Alsatian-type animals.

Commonly, they are believed to be death omens, although this theory is changeable as certain individuals claim that the beasts have offered protection to travellers as they walk or cycle along rural back lanes towards their destination.

These elusive sprits go by numerous names such as Hell Hounds, Black Dogs, Barguest, Padfoot and many more. In Yorkshire, they are commonly referred to as Black Shuck.

Many believe that the mysterious beasts spotted around the UK reflect the beliefs of the ancient pagan past: memories of the many deities that had a powerful responsibility for a certain thing. The greatest of all the pagan gods was Woden, after which Wednesday is named. This epic sky god was said to ride into battle upon an eight-legged steed, accompanied by his ferociously powerful pack of black dogs. In Greek mythology, Hades was said to have his own pet beast named Cerberus, who was the guardian of the underworld.

Regardless of overall appearance, they all seem to share demonic eyes (either black or red and resembling hot burning coals) large, razor-sharp teeth and a mouth dripping with foam and saliva.

These mysterious dogs are also tied in with the folklore surrounding demonic pacts. These are deals that are made with the devil and grant a wish in return for one's soul. These legends have been around ever since religion began: the famous German tales of Faust tell of the story around the turn of the sixteenth century.

Interestingly, it wasn't until the Robert Johnson legend became well known that the spectral dogs were introduced into these pacts. Robert was a blues singer who died at the young age of just 27. He was reported to have openly told family and friends that he'd sold his soul to the devil in exchange for his musical talents, and his songs showcase a wide array of occult references such as 'hell hound on my trail' and 'crossroad blues'.

As the legend goes, he died choking on his own blood and muttering words about black dogs that have been chasing him, despite being the only one that could see or hear them at the time.

Over the years, there have been hundreds of people claiming to have encountered these elusive beasts which generally will do one of two things: they will either fill the person with a sense of safety and accompany them to their destination, or they will fill them with fear and scare them away from a specific location.

Of course, these are only the tales of those who have lived to tell them. As to whether or not they can indeed snatch the soul of a sinner and drag them down to the fiery pits of hell is something we cannot possibly know until our own time of judgement arrives.

Due to the polar-opposite way in which they are said to protect as much as scare, there are certain people who believe that these dogs are not even demonic or hellish at all, but rather a form of a protective angel that is sent to guide and watch over certain individuals. This is not a popular opinion of them, yet it's interesting that for as many stories from people claiming to have been chased by a large black dog with burning eyes and foaming mouth, whilst experiencing an intense feeling of dread, there are equally as many stories from witnesses claiming to have been accompanied by this beast, often whilst either walking or cycling along rural lanes at night.

These individuals claim to have felt safe and comforted in the phantom's company before it ran away into the wilderness once they had reached their destination. Both examples are showcased in the Hall Lane tale in the West Yorkshire section.

With such vague folklore surrounding them, it's hard to determine what these animals actually are, but given so many alleged sightings, it does pose the question: are they real? Perhaps there are many variations that look alike and that is why so many of the tales contradict each other. Perhaps only Hell Hounds can snatch the souls of sinners before dragging them down to the fiery pits of hell whilst spectral black dogs are indeed omens of some kind.

Or just maybe, they are simply everyday sightings of wild animals that have taken on a life of their own over time.

8

East Yorkshire

Annison Funeral Parlour, Hull

It would be wrong to create a book about Yorkshire hauntings without starting our easterly adventure at the infamous Annison Funeral Parlour, a building that has had various uses over the years, from a photographer's shop to a prison, a place bursting at the seams with well-documented paranormal phenomena.

Amongst the alleged paranormal phenomena that resides within the creepy building, the ghostly cries of the Catholics that were tortured and murdered here by Protestants back when it was a prison can be heard echoing around the rooms, and loud footsteps and disembodied whistling are often heard around the old livery that would have been used to store the horses responsible for transporting the bodies when it was a funeral home.

Many witnesses claim to have encountered a ghostly man, crawling along the floor of the livery, accompanied by strange shadows that can be seen wandering the building after dark. It's believed the man was a Catholic, desperately trying to escape from the apparitions of the Protestants that are still searching for him in the afterlife.

Amid the endless tales of paranormal phenomena, the most intriguing story is that of Mary Jane Langley, also said to haunt the building after her tragic demise at the end of the nine-teenth century.

Mary Jane was just 18 years old when she visited the building that, at the time, was a photographer's shop. After having her photograph taken, she left, never to be seen alive again. Her corpse was discovered a few hours later, on 30 July 1891, as she'd been dumped on Long Lane in the nearby village of Preston, after having had her throat slit by her murderer.

A farce of a police investigation quickly followed, with numerous locals being accused of the crime but, alas, no one was ever charged with the murder of Mary Jane Langley.

Many people believed that Mary was a victim of Frederick Bailey Deeming, an ex-sailor who had traded his sea legs for a life of crime and murder. Deeming already had form, as he'd killed his own family in the same manner months before the murder of Mary Jane. He was so prolific that some even believe he may have been Jack the Ripper. The fact that he was recently released from a Hull prison prior to Mary's killing spurred on those believing him to be responsible.

Mary's ghost has been seen numerous times in Annison Funeral Parlour, but the question is, why? She would have been excited for her visit as in 1891, not everyone could simply afford to have their photograph taken and it was, by all accounts, something of a rare treat that she'd looked forward to for many weeks prior to her visit.

Other than that, she was not killed within the building and had no prior connections to it so perhaps, being her last happy memory, that is the reason her spirit is said to still haunt the Annison Funeral Parlour to this day.

The fact that the alleged hauntings are in an old funeral home might be enough suggestion for people to expect to see spirits there. The close proximity to the road and pavements outside could be responsible for the ghostly sounds when combined with the acoustic nature of the building, particularly the large, empty, old stables that echo any small sounds beyond their usual capacity.

Although macabre, it's unlikely that any funeral home would actually be haunted by any of the cadavers that rested within them prior to their burial or cremation, as they did not die in the building or, in most cases, were even aware of its existence.

That being said, the most likely spirits that would haunt this location are the Catholics that were tortured and killed on location, but if they are the only spectral beings within the walls, why has Mary Jane herself been spotted on numerous occasions?

Do the restless spirits of these unfortunates truly haunt the eerie building in East Yorkshire to this very day? Or have the legends, combined with the macabre nature of the building, created the belief of such entities? Is the girl who has been spotted truly Mary Jane Langley? Or is it another sad tale that has been lost over time, overshadowed by the murder case?

It is strange that so many different paranormal groups have visited the location overnight, yet all seem to experience the same phenomena. Could it simply be the natural noises of the outside world playing tricks on suggestible minds? Or are the echoes of the past truly imprinted on the fabric of time at Annison Funeral Parlour?

All Saints' Church, Pocklington

A cross inscribed AD 627 within the grounds of All Saints' Church dates the worship that takes place here back to the Anglo-Saxon times. However, the oldest parts of the current building date back to the thirteenth century.

Another notable plaque at this location commemorates the life of Thomas Pelling, who both died and was buried within the grounds of this eerie location within just four days. It is because of that man that one of the strangest phantoms imaginable is still alleged to haunt the churchyard to this day.

All Saints' Church at Pocklington, the final resting place of the Birdman.

There have been numerous reports of a winged creature, often mistaken for a demon or other insidious entity, flying through the night sky, and it is said to manifest within the old churchyard in Pocklington and fly amongst the graves.

Intrigued by this strange tale, I set about looking for eyewitness accounts and was inundated with people claiming to have seen the so-called flying demon. Amongst the tales of those hearing his laughter or claiming to have spotted him through the trees, I found a local man named William Skipper, who has lived in that area for his entire life. William claimed to have come face to face with the beast on an autumn night in 2008, and he kindly met with me to share his truly horrifying, yet strangely enchanting story:

> I was passing the churchyard one evening on my way home from the pub, when I heard a strange flapping sound, much like the noise a kite makes when flying on a windy day. Intrigued as to what it was, I wandered through the gates of the churchyard and listened as it got louder and louder, the closer I got.
>
> For a second, I wondered if it was a flag, but there wasn't any wind. As I approached the church itself, suddenly a strange shadow appeared in the night sky that seemed to be flying in circles above the graves. I was strangely intrigued by what appeared to be a thick wisp of smoke and watched on curiously, but within seconds, curiosity turned to fear as it flew straight at me.
>
> The noise seemed to be coming directly from the thing, as if clothing was flapping as it flew through the sky, but I couldn't see a body let alone any clothes. Strangely, I could clearly see a man's face at the top of the smoke-like mist.
>
> I turned and ran as fast as I could, as it followed me towards the gates, circling around my body whenever it got close. As I finally ran out of the gates, I heard a man laughing as clear as day, from the churchyard, but when I looked back it had vanished and I was all alone.
>
> I told my wife and a close friend, and we all came back to investigate that same evening, but it was gone. They thought I'd had one too many that night and had imagined the whole thing, but I know what I saw at All Saints' Church and I'm certain it was the Bird Man.

William's story is bizarre, but it becomes even stranger when the history of the building is researched. In the eighteenth century, a man named Thomas Pelling made a living as a regular daredevil, performing impossible feats that defied gravity by jumping up to, and down from, some of the highest buildings in the land.

Pelling used a series of ropes and cables as winches that hoisted him up and allowed him to seemingly fly back down to earth. His act proved to be very popular and he travelled the country performing to astounded crowds of people that flocked to witness the Bird Man in action.

On 10 April 1733, Thomas Pelling brought his act to the village of Pocklington and, in usual fashion, crowds of paying spectators came out to watch his amazing performance. Sadly for Thomas, on that particular night one of his assistants made a fatal error by not tightening a safety rope that he would use to ascend from the tower of the church.

As hordes of excited fans watched on, the Bird Man fell from the sky, screaming as he plummeted to his death. He was buried in the church grounds under the spot of the impact, where a plaque remains to this day, commemorating his life.

Some of the older graves in All Saints' Church, said to be Thomas Pelling's favourite to fly around.

Around Pocklington, the tale of Thomas Pelling is a common one and it's unlikely there's a resident in the village that doesn't know it. Pocklington even hosts its own Flying Man Festival each year to both raise funds and keep this historical story alive.

With that being said, could William's story be the product of his prior knowledge, mixed with the alcohol he'd consumed that evening? Could the numerous tales from other people, claiming to have seen the manifestation of the Bird Man, also be rationally explained? Or maybe, the ghost of Thomas Pelling is still performing his amazing act in the afterlife, now safe in the knowledge that safety ropes are no longer required.

Hull Road, Keyingham

The A1033 in East Yorkshire is the home of a sad apparition that has been seen many, many times over the years. Appearing on cold and often foggy nights, the spectre is that of a young woman, cradling her tiny baby in her arms.

It is believed that this phantom is the restless spirit of Betty Edwards, a young lady who was tragically murdered in the mid-eighteenth century. Betty was just 17 at the time of her death; her baby of just two months was the illicit daughter of a local wealthy man. He shunned the pair and threatened Betty should she ever speak a word of their affair.

Feeling alone and vulnerable, the new mother stole a few coins from the man before making her way towards Hull where she hoped to start a better life for her child.

Sadly for Betty, she was spotted in the act of stealing and in an even worse twist of the tale, her spectator was none other than a highwayman, posing as a weary traveller.

He followed the pair as they walked along the roads and waited for his perfect moment. As they were out of sight of any witnesses and with no other carriages coming their way, the highwayman stopped Betty and demanded that she hand over the coins.

Betty refused and struggled with her assailant whilst still cradling the baby in her arms. During the commotion, a knife was drawn by the man, most likely in an attempt to scare her into handing over the money.

Still refusing, she battled on some more before the knife pierced her skin and she fell to the floor, the baby still clutched tightly in her arms.

The highwayman made a dash for it and must have been remorseful, as when she was found soon after, she still had the coins in her possession. The baby was unharmed and brought up by a local family in Keyingham. The highwayman was never caught, but with Betty's dying breaths she told the family who took the baby everything.

The wealthy man had already told the village that he'd been robbed, so when the family arrived back with Mary's corpse, the babe in arms and the missing money, everyone figured out who the baby truly belonged to and the wealthy man's wife left with most of his fortune.

To this day, reports of a White Lady wandering that stretch of road, holding a newborn baby, are reported on a regular basis. The story has become something of a local folk legend over the years and certainly offers an enchanting tale. But is there any truth to the it? Or are the sightings simply the product of overactive imaginations and attention-seeking minds?

St Andrew's Church, Bainton

The current church of St Andrew dates back to the fourteenth century, although worship has taken place at the location since the Anglo-Saxon times.

With a church of this age stories are usually a given, and St Andrew's is no exception. Locals tell us of a hooded figure,

The old graves at St. Andrew's church that the Black Shuck is often spotted guarding.

accompanied by a large black dog, often spotted patrolling the graveyard at night – a phenomenon that many people claim to have witnessed.

The animal is said to be about 4ft tall with jet black hair and piercing red eyes. Given the area's alleged ties to witchcraft in the mid-fifteenth century, the hooded phantom and his Shuck are said to guard the building and churchyard that folklore states is the gateway to the underworld.

The beast is said to wander the graveyard under the supervision of its ghostly master, watching over the dead and keeping unwanted intruders out. There have even been claims that the elusive animal has been spotted at funerals within the grounds, as if waiting to escort the soul of the deceased into the afterlife, once his mortal body has been laid to rest.

A local paranormal group decided to investigate the claims back in 2009 and, although they never actually saw the animal, many members claimed to have felt hot breath on their faces during vigils, accompanied with a stench described like 'the rotting corpses of a thousand bodies'.

They also claimed to have captured a number of ghostly shadows lurking within the churchyard that evening although, as with all paranormal evidence, the pictures are not clear and therefore open to interpretation.

The group also said they saw the hooded apparition wander through the graves before disappearing through the locked door of the church itself. Whilst the pictures they presented are interesting, I feel pareidolia may have played its part amongst this group of seasoned believers. The shadows are too obscure to discount branches, leaves and clouds being the culprits.

When the group left the site and analysed their data, they also caught on tape a haunting sound that echoed across the night sky, resembling that of a wolf howling. Self-proclaimed psychics within the group claimed to be able to see the red eyes of the animal, which they said was there to protect the eternal resting place of the dead.

A previous vicar at the church commented on the various phenomena:

> Whilst I have never seen the hound or hooded figure in question, there is a strange feeling of being watched whilst in the churchyard, irrelevant if it's day or night. I can say that on occasion, I have heard what sounded like a dog howling, although it may well have been from someone's pet in the village. Do I think the place is haunted? I don't know, I don't think so. But who knows?

It's hard to determine if St Andrew's Church is indeed haunted by a mysterious hooded figure and what can only be described as Black Shuck. It's fair to say that local superstition has played its part but that doesn't rule out the phenomena.

Either way, the darkness, combined with the eerie look of the church, make it a place not for the faint-hearted and, with over thirty individual witness accounts, it's quite possible that something unearthly may be lurking within the shadows of the old church grounds.

Osbourne Street, Hull

During the nineteenth century, the most despicable trend of murdering any unwanted children was rife around Great Britain, with some of the most horrific cases occurring in Hull. Amidst the stomach-churning tales of mothers who hanged, poisoned and drowned their defenceless young infants, is the gruesome case of Jane Crompton.

To the world, Crompton seemed a relatively normal woman, a loving wife and doting mother – but to those who knew her more personally, it was clear she was unhinged.

She was often reported to say that she hated her youngest child and wished that she had never been born. A week or so before the murder, a friend was allegedly told, 'I shall have to do something to my baby, I cannot do anything with it.'

On 15 May 1873, Jane Crompton had finally had enough of her 4-month-old baby Sarah Alice, and whilst her 3-year-old watched on, she cut at the baby's throat with a kitchen knife until the head came loose, decapitating the child in the most horrific way.

Crompton then took her 3-year-old to a neighbour's house before going to the local police station to confess. As the authorities rushed to 65 Osbourne Street, they found the baby's bloody body, a foot or so away from its discarded head. Her short trial ended in a whole life sentence and she died in the newly built HMP Hull, 2 miles east of the city centre.

The area of the murder has since become a paranormal hot-spot, as paranormal investigators flock to try and get a glimpse of the infamous Black Lady that haunts that place, believed to be the soulless spirit of Jane Crompton.

There is a local saying that 'curiosity takes you to a graveyard, but foolishness takes you to Osbourne Street', referring to the paranormal investigators who are said to be risking their lives whenever they attempt to contact the infamous Black Lady.

Sharon White attended a paranormal investigation in the area in 2014 and ever since that fateful night, she hasn't returned. This is her story in unedited form:

> We were all pretty excited about our visit to Osbourne Street, as it was reportedly one of the most haunted places in Hull. The only problem at the time was, I didn't really know how it had got that title.
>
> It wasn't because of the volume of sightings or paranormal activity as you'd expect, but instead because of the violent way in which the Black Lady was said to appear, although it has to be said, it's a rare phenomenon and only a handful of people ever have actually seen her as a full-bodied apparition.
>
> On that night, we held a vigil on the street at around midnight, but nothing happened. Hull's a busy place, so it was difficult trying to communicate in a built-up area with the usual noises you'd expect to hear.
>
> About an hour or so later, we were all ready for heading back, when suddenly someone shouted that they could see a shadow. I looked over and right there in the street was the Black Lady. There was absolutely no mistaking what it was.
>
> I froze to the spot in fear, but some of the other investigators edged closer and tried to communicate. As they did, the shadow shot towards one of the team members and it looked as though it pushed him to the ground. He fell back, cracking his head on the concrete so hard that he later needed stitches.
>
> We all bolted away as fast as we could, and I've never been back ever since. I'm certain the legends of the Black Lady are true, and it was her that we saw that night whilst investigating on Osbourne Street.

Sharon's account is certainly terrifying, but it's interesting that she referred to the phantom as the Black Lady. I asked her afterwards if she was familiar with the tale of Jane Crompton and surprisingly, she wasn't. I found this most strange as traditionally, the legend of the Black Lady stemmed from the horrific tale of the child murderer.

Unfortunately, the paranormal group that Sharon had visited with has now disbanded and I was unable to track down any former members. You'd have to assume they were familiar with the history, nonetheless.

To break down the account from a parapsychological point of view, it's possible that the street lamps created the shadow that the group mistook for the Black Lady. In addition, as they edged closer the light dynamic would have changed, which could have caused the shadow to appear as though it was moving, possibly in the group's direction.

The paranormal investigator who was allegedly pushed may have just been startled upon seeing the strange phenomenon in front of him, causing him to step back and lose his footing, resulting in his injury. As for the stitches, Sharon admits that she wasn't present at the hospital after the incident and heard this from others.

Science and reason aside however, is it feasible to assume that an infamous Black Lady really does haunt Osbourne Street in Hull? And if so, is it possible that she may, in fact, be the ghostly entity of Jane Crompton? If any lessons are to be learnt from this tale, tread carefully. You never truly know what forces you might be investigating.

Northgate, Cottingham

The infamous sighting of the Black Shuck that is said to roam Northgate has been reported numerous times over the years. Local animal charities claim they have been called out to the area in search of a large stray dog on more than ten different occasions.

The first sighting of the mysterious beast was reported by none other than an officer of the law in the 1980s.

The policeman was patrolling Cottingham one evening when he wandered along Northgate. As he neared the halfway point of the busy road, a large black dog allegedly jumped out in front of him from an alleyway between the shops.

The constable froze to the spot as the dog stared him in the eyes, its razor-sharp teeth glistening under the street lights. After a few moments, the officer started to ease away and, as he got about 20ft away from the animal, he claims that it started to fade away slowly before disappearing altogether, right in front of his eyes.

In fear, he turned to run and at that moment, he heard tyres screeching along Northgate as a car lost control on the damp road. Turning to see the commotion, he witnessed the car as it skidded for a few seconds before colliding with a brick wall, tragically killing both the driver and his girlfriend instantly.

The officer firmly believes that, had the dog not stopped him in his tracks, he would have been approximately at the point at which the crash occurred, most likely killing him too. He believed that the mysterious apparition of the elusive black dog saved his life that day and, despite the fear that washed over him upon first seeing the animal, he was thankful for the strange experience.

Since that fateful night, there have been many sightings along this stretch of road, all of which tell a similar story of a large black dog, appearing as if from nowhere, before running away or vanishing into thin air. None of the tales are similar to the way in which the hound seemingly delayed the spectator, saving them from a tragic accident or injury.

I searched for eyewitness accounts and was introduced to Peter Garvey, a local engineer who was walking along Northgate in 2013. Peter claimed to have encountered the animal on a damp cold night, similar to the one in the 1980s. This is his story:

> I was walking along Northgate on my way to see a friend as I did almost every Saturday evening. It was very quiet, hardly any cars on the road, and I remember thinking it made a nice change.

As I walked along the road, suddenly this giant dog stepped out of a gap and stood staring at me. It didn't bark or growl, it just stood still. I remember thinking two things. Firstly, 'look at the bloody size of that!' and secondly, that its tail was still which I didn't think was a good thing. It certainly didn't look like it wanted to play.

I turned and sprinted back in the direction I'd come from and it followed for a few feet before turning around and running off. I went the long way round to my friends that night but have continued to walk along Northgate ever since. I've never seen hide nor hair of it since, though.

I honestly don't know if it was what you'd call a spectral dog, but I've never seen anything as big in my entire life.

The obvious question remains, is there really a Black Shuck wandering Northgate in Cottingham? You might argue that the phenomenon was little more than a domesticated animal that had escaped during the night. You could suggest that the fatigued officer, working late one evening, simply imagined the tale that has now taken on a life of its own as the folklore legend spreads. Or perhaps a demonic Shuck truly is lurking in the shadows of Cottingham.

But with the sheer number of sightings that far outlive the lifespan of a single dog, could it be that an infamous supernatural Black Dog truly is roaming the streets of Cottingham in East Yorkshire?

Saltmarshe Hall, Howden

The land and buildings were originally gifted to Sir Lionel Saltmarshe in 1067, after he was knighted by William the Conqueror following the Norman Conquest. Over the years, the original design has been altered and added to, creating the beautiful gardens and grand structure that stand today.

The home was owned by the same family for a remarkable 900 years before the line died out in the 1970s. It is now owned by the Whyte family, who have renovated the property and made it available for the public to visit or hold events such as weddings.

Amidst the grandeur of the house, set inside some 17 acres of picturesque land, strange tales of ghostly goings-on are reported on a regular basis, and terrifying tales of strange shadows, loud footsteps and disembodied voices are quite common within Saltmarshe Hall.

The building is set upon a large network of underground tunnels that would have been used during the Victorian period, allowing servants to move to various areas around the home without interrupting the family or guests. These tunnels and cellars are almost exactly as they would have been when in use, and they are still home to some of the items that would have been transported along the dark passageways, such as cutlery, wine bottles and goblets.

The wine cellar is reportedly haunted by a maid who can be regularly seen rummaging around as if looking for a lost bottle. She appears as a full-bodied apparition but seems unaware of the world around her.

The passageways are said to be the home of numerous entities including that of a man who is said to shout and charge at people in an aggressive manner if disturbed. It's not clear who he was in life as the servants wouldn't have dared act in this manner whilst working in Saltmarshe Hall.

Countless shadows have been witnessed, floating around the eerie underground corridors, and ghostly cries from within the stone walls are often accompanied by the putrid stench of death and rotting flesh. These follow suit from other tales of people being murdered and sealed behind the brickwork but, given the history of the place, it's highly unlikely at this location.

Outside the building, the ghostly apparition of a woman in white has been reported multiple times. She is said to float between the pond and the stables that were erected in 1842.

No one knows for sure who this lady was either, but she was believed to have been a member of the family in life.

The north wing of the building was abandoned in the 1930s as the war forced many of the servants to leave, and it's only recently that renovations have started to transform the wing back into a habitable area. This is by far the hotspot of the paranormal phenomena but is that because it was abandoned for so long that it looks eerie enough to house spirits?

Strange ghostly whistling is often heard in this part of the building and the figure of a lady, who appears to be intoxicated, manifests in front of unsuspecting visitors before shouting at them and disappearing into thin air.

A ghostly poltergeist is also said to haunt the north wing, with numerous witnesses reporting to have had things thrown at them by an unseen hand, along with doors opening before being slammed shut and a man's laughter that echoes around the wing at night.

With the River Ouse running close to the property and many paranormal investigators' claims that the water acts as a catalyst for paranormal phenomena, could it be that in fact the effects of the river, combined with pareidolia, are causing the strange events that are experienced within Saltmarshe Hall?

Are the distant sounds of the river entering the building before echoing around the walls? Is the excess vapour causing people to believe they are seeing shadows when in fact it's little more than mist? Is the putrid stench in the cellars simply rotting earth that is carried by the damp soil?

Or are the ghostly apparitions of previous servants, guests and family members truly haunting this eerie place to this very day, unaware of the changing world around them and still trapped in the era of their deaths?

Coppleflat Lane, Beverley

One of the strangest tales that Yorkshire has to offer has to be the curious story of the phantom hotel. If you were to search the internet for this grand place or even drive along Coppleflat Lane, the chances are you wouldn't be able to find it. But why is that?

Perhaps it's such an amazing hotel, so exclusive to the rich and famous that general advertising isn't required. Maybe its quaint ways of the past have separated it from our modern technological world, or maybe, it never really existed in the first place.

For centuries there have been folk tales all over the globe from people claiming to have chanced upon a grand hotel that almost appeared to be within the wrong time period: the hospitality, the price, the room and everything else in between. It's also always claimed to have been the best place the guests have ever stayed in, yet when they try to tell friends about this amazing guest house or drive back to the location at which they assumed it to be, the building has vanished with no record of a similar one within the area.

These stories are personal favourites of mine and I love the air of romance associated with these creepy tales. Throughout history, many people have claimed to have encountered this bizarre phenomenon, at the time assuming nothing to be strange other than the style that transports guests back to a bygone era.

Sydney in 1904, Texas in 1919, Scotland 1947, Russia 1956, the list of alleged sightings is endless, and one of these strange tales occurred right here in East Yorkshire back in 1997.

Alex Pickerington, a banker from Hull, was driving along Coppleflat Lane one evening when his car broke down in the middle of a violent storm. With his phone not working on account of the moisture it had absorbed, and stranded in the middle of nowhere, Alex started walking along the road, using

The area on Coppleflat Lane where the phantom hotel was alleged to have appeared.

his jacket to shield himself from the violent rain that battered his face and body.

As he walked out of sight of the hazard lights flashing on his car, he noticed a brightly lit building in front of him on that stretch of road. Rushing over to take cover from the storm, Alex ran inside the hotel and asked to use the phone. He claimed the lady on the reception desk was a young woman who was quite normal, but the reception felt very old-fashioned. Upon asking if he could use the telephone, the lady informed Alex that the storm had knocked out all of the cables and that a generator was providing power to the building.

With no other option, Alex handed the woman a credit card and asked for a room for the night, but as the woman handed him his key, she told him the card was not needed yet. Still unaware of anything strange, he thanked her and made his way up the stairs of the 1950s-themed guest house.

He stated that, as he walked past the first landing, he saw three men chatting on the hallway. They wore striped shirts with red braces, and each sported a fedora-style hat, looking something like the mobsters in the old-fashioned movies.

As he arrived in his room, it was beyond perfect. The bed was gigantic and the pillows and quilt were perfectly fluffy. There was tea and coffee accompanied by delicious ginger biscuits and free TV channels, although the old set was black and white.

Alex said that after showering, he got dressed and returned to the bar area, sitting amongst the other guests, all of whom looked out of place in the same way the three men on the landing did.

He ordered a steak pie and chips, but said the meal was more like a mini banquet and could have fed three people. It was far too big for him, so he finished what he could before enjoying a couple of drinks in the bar and chatting with other guests. The conversation wasn't out of the ordinary; topics such as the storm and the food were exchanged in a few short words. One thing that did catch his eye was the way people seemed to stare at his suit as if they wanted to enquire about it.

The next morning, the sun was shining, and he went down to pay his bill and return to his car. The lady on reception informed him that she'd already rung for assistance and that he should wait by his vehicle. Generously, or so he thought at the time, the receptionist told Alex there was no charge for the room, nor the food or drinks he'd consumed the previous evening. Although this was very strange, Alex surmised that it was merely a charitable gesture for his night of being caught in the storm.

He returned to his car and the recovery van arrived around fifteen minutes later. His car was fixed at the roadside and he told the mechanic about the chance night he'd experienced, but the man wasn't aware of any hotels in the area. Alex got back in the driver's seat and drove along the lane, passing the spot where he'd stayed the previous night but, after driving along the same stretch of road five times, it was nowhere to be seen.

Since that strange night, he's asked numerous friends and family but again, the location of the 1950s-themed hotel remains a mystery. After spending a long time wondering if he'd simply made a mistake, Alex now firmly believes that he did in fact stop the night in a phantom hotel, and ever since that fateful evening, he's read up religiously on the occult and other alleged experiences similar to that of his own.

Over the years, the occult has been tied in with hotels in many books, symbolising a secret place for infidelity, an escape from the real world, a place where guests can reinvent themselves as anyone in a place of complete strangers, or a purgatory. Perhaps these are amongst the reasons why so many phantom hotels have been reported over the years in numerous places around the globe.

They are often tied in with electrical storms, the theory being that ghosts use energy to manifest, so it stands to reason to assume that during any electrical storms, spirits would be able to manifest with ease.

But is that to say Alex's bizarre tale has any truth to it? Was the hotel simply the fabrication of an overworked mind? Perhaps he was elsewhere and needed to think of an excuse fast, the hotel being the only thing that would come out of his lips.

Maybe, he slept in his car that evening and dreamt the whole episode. Or maybe one of the oldest phenomena in the world did indeed visit East Yorkshire on a stormy night in 1997.

Milners Row, Skelton

Just east of Saltmarshe Hall lies Milners Row in Skelton, running adjacent to the River Ouse. Milners Row is a picturesque lane that offers stunning views of both the river and the aesthetically pleasing cottages running alongside.

Many people choose to walk or jog along the pathways running by it but for some, a stroll along the scenic paths can turn into a terrifying account of paranormal phenomena.

There have been many reports of a young girl, wandering along the riverside wearing old-fashioned, rag-styled clothing. She casually meanders along the verge, often picking flowers or playing dandelion clocks by blowing the heads from the dead flowers.

Numerous people have approached the girl, wondering if she might be lost given her young age and shabby appearance. Others quietly watch on from a distance, waiting for her parents to come into view.

After wandering for a few minutes, the spectral being is said to do one of three things. Sometimes she simply sits on the grass bank before slowly vanishing into thin air. Other times she runs out of sight, never to be seen by the same spectator twice. Her third and final way of exiting is rather more disturbing – She either falls or jumps into the river before splashing around whilst fighting for her life. It's such a vivid apparition that, on occasion, the police have been called to investigate, only to find no trace of the spirit.

As mentioned previously, many paranormal investigators claim that water can act as a catalyst for paranormal events and it's possible that this unfortunate girl may have drowned in the River Ouse in years gone by.

With both of these factors considered, is it possible that the little girl is recreating her final moments in the afterlife?

Perhaps trapped in her own purgatory as she's always spotted alone and never with her parents.

Or could it just be the product of folklore and imagination fused together with the enchantingly beautiful look of the area that causes such tales to manifest?

Chalk Pits, Flamborough

This unusual piece of folklore dates back to the mid-eighteenth century and tells an eerie tale of a woman with an equally eerie name, Jenny Gallows. It was said that Jenny had discovered that her husband had been having an affair with a local girl and, in a fit of rage, she brutally bludgeoned the girl to death in a nearby stable.

Upon discovering what she had done, her husband raced to report the murder to the authorities, leaving Jenny alone as the realisation of her actions slowly dawned upon her.

Fearing for her own life, she fled Flamborough and headed to the Chalk Pits, but it's unclear what her intentions were at the time.

A traveller claimed to watch on as the young woman sat on the edge of a cliff for some time, gazing out at the water with a blank stare. As the man decided to approach the woman, she stood up and smiled to herself before holding up her arms and simply falling into the abyss, her body plummeting down to the rocks beneath and killing her instantly.

The man rushed to Flamborough to report the incident and the body was quickly identified as that of Jenny Gallows, proving the tale that her husband had given the police to be true.

To this day, the Chalk Pits remain a beautiful yet strange place to visit and you can almost feel the energy of Jenny and the many others like her who would have plummeted to their deaths at the location. Unlike the other cadavers, however, Jenny is still said to haunt the area to this very day.

A folk tale tells that if you circle the pits eight times, her spirit will rise up and show herself to anyone brave enough to accept the challenge. In 1912, a farmer decided to participate in the legend and circled the area eight times on horseback.

With his task finished, he claimed the ghost of Jenny Gallows did indeed rise up out of the pits before charging towards him at pace and with clear anger at being disturbed during her eternal slumber.

The farmer said that he rode back to Flamborough as quickly as his horse would allow, but the spirit followed relentlessly before getting close enough to the horse that it was actually able to bite it on the hide. From that day, the animal had a strange white patch upon its croup that remained until the day it died.

Whilst there have been numerous other tales of people attempting to invoke the restless spirit of Jenny Gallows, no one has ever experienced such a horrifyingly bizarre tale as the farmer in 1912. Others have claimed to have seen her spirit or heard her crying around the area at dusk however, and there have even been several sightings of a phantom lady sitting by the cliff side before vanishing into thin air in this apocryphal yet charming tale of the Chalk Pits at Flamborough.

St Michael's Church, Bempton

Used as a place of worship since AD 600, parts of the current church date back to the thirteenth century and, as with most ancient burial sites that come complete with folklore of ghostly goings-on, St Michael's Church in Bempton is no exception.

Many parishioners claim to have seen the spectral, shadowy figure of a large man along with the figure of a young girl, often spotted running and playing between the gravestones, accompanied by a strong scent of rose petals. Others have heard the girl laughing and singing childhood songs in the rear of the church itself, but they have never caught a glimpse of the spirit responsible.

A local folk tale tells of a little girl who wandered out of a Sunday service in 1936. Upon discovering his daughter had left the church, her father went outside to find her and scold her for, once again, leaving the service.

As the man wandered outside, he let out a loud cry as he stumbled upon the limp and lifeless body of his daughter. She'd fallen from a tree in the church grounds and broken her neck, which killed her instantly. It is this unfortunate girl's spirit that is believed to haunt the graveyard to this day.

On a couple of occasions, witnesses have claimed to have approached the little girl believing her to be lost, before she hides behind a headstone and vanishes from sight. Within the walls of the church, there is an old doorway that has since been bricked up although its location can clearly be seen. Both parishioners and former vicars also claim to have seen a large shadow, around 7ft tall, wander the church before exiting through the door that perhaps was in use during their mortal time on this earth.

Many believe this figure to be that of a monk returning to the nearby abbey after visiting the church, whilst others consider it could be the father of the girl trying to find her in the afterlife.

Alice Burrows, a local resident, was leaving flowers at her father's grave when she claimed to have experienced the strange phenomenon. This is her story:

It was a normal day, cold and cloudy, and I went to put the flowers on my dad's grave as I did every couple of weeks or so.

I heard a young child giggling and as I looked up, she was peeking at me over the top of a large headstone about 20 feet from my dad's spot. I smiled at the girl as she looked over at me. Her eyes twinkled, and I knew she was smiling back, despite only being able to see her eyes and the top of her head.

I finished tending to the grave and smiled again before leaving. The girl was still in the same spot. As I took a few steps towards the exit, I realised I'd not seen any other adults in the churchyard so thought I should check if she was okay. I turned to where she was, but she'd gone. I looked amongst the graves and around the church, but she was nowhere to be seen. I've since heard the stories, but I don't know what to think really. She didn't look like a spirit, she looked as real as you or I.

Alice's tale could be interesting if you think the girl she saw was indeed the apparition of the young lady that tragically lost her life here. Of course, it's possible that she was just a regular girl who was playing close by at the time but, as with all paranormal stories, it's a question of what you believe. Whatever your thoughts on the subject, it would appear that St Michael's Church may be home to more than meets the eye.

Burton Agnes Hall, Driffield

Dating back to 1173, parts of the original Norman manor house are still in use today. Amid the history that surrounds the building and the later constructed hall, numerous ghost stories have developed over the years.

Disembodied cries that echo around the rooms, footsteps stomping up and down the staircase in the dead of night and the laughter of spirit children playing in the dining room are amongst some of the strange phenomena said to reside within the manor house and hall.

But it's another legend that really separates Burton Agnes Hall from the paranormal pack, so to speak. A legend that dates back to 1620, when the hall itself was built by the noble Griffith family – a legend so strange, so enchantingly unbelievable, that it marks the perfect way to end our East Yorkshire journey.

It was said that, like most children, Sir Henry Griffith's daughter Anne was particularly excited to move into their new family home near Driffield. After waiting ten years for the construction to be completed, the family finally left the manor house next door and moved into Burton Agnes Hall.

Sadly, a short while after moving into their new home, Anne was visiting family in nearby Harpham when she was attacked and robbed as she made the journey back to Burton Agnes Hall. She stumbled home, both battered and bruised, before her sisters looked after her by the bedside, tending to the critical wounds that she'd received. As the life slowly dwindled from the girl, she told her sisters that she wanted them to cut the head from her body after her death and place it in the new home that she loved so dearly. The sisters agreed to this request in a bid to comfort the dying girl and shortly afterwards she was dead.

The local parson conducted Anne Griffith's funeral and she was laid to rest, as expected, in the churchyard over from Burton Agnes Hall. Within just a few days of her burial, strange things started to happen in the building. Books were thrown from the shelves, doors were opened and slammed shut by an unseen hand, and ghostly screams were reported in the dead of night, along with the shadowy figure believed to be the restless spirit of Anne.

The family were so concerned by the events that they arranged for their daughter's corpse to be exhumed and the head to be sealed behind a wall in the great hall, as per her dying wish. With this task completed, the phenomena ceased.

It was reported that numerous sceptical servants and guests made attempts at finding the skull that was said to be concealed behind the wall above the great hall, to reveal the tale as little more than a myth. But every attempt was greeted with ghostly cries, objects being thrown around the room or the transparent manifestation of a spirit believed to have been the ghost of Anne Griffith.

Nearly 200 years later, another ancestor of Anne moved into the house and upon hearing the tale, ordered for the skull to be removed and returned to the churchyard. Obviously, the macabre image of a skull sealed within the walls of his newly inherited home was not to his liking.

When the skull was discovered and removed, the hauntings started once again, far more violent in nature this time around. It was said that objects were thrown directly at people within Burton Agnes Hall and the manifestations were more vivid in appearance, actually attacking anyone who came into contact with them.

Burning logs were also thrown out of the fire by an unseen hand and numerous family members and guests reported waking up with deep scratches that they had gained during the night. After a short while, the new owner ordered for the skull to be replaced and, once again, the hauntings stopped.

The macabre item is still said to be walled up within Burton Agnes Hall and there is a large portrait of Anne and her sisters currently in the inner hall that, legend says, watches for anyone inclined to remove the skull for a third time.

An American woman, visiting family in Driffield in 2005, visited the hall and experienced a strange tale that is one of many common accounts reported within this historical location. This is Nichola Oxley's story:

I decided to visit the Burton Agnes Hall as I was visiting family close by and was interested in the history of the place, being a foreigner visiting England. I was alone at the time and gazing upon the items within the building and imagining living there in times gone by, as I'm sure many guests do.

All was very normal until I was about to leave. I heard someone crying behind me and turned to see a lady in a white dress. She didn't look like a ghost – in fact I thought she was a real woman at first. I walked over to see if she was okay and, at that moment, she turned to me and then vanished right before my eyes. I was so scared that I ran out of the hall but as I did, I saw some children in the corner of my eye, about five or six of them at a guess.

As quickly as I turned to look, they too had disappeared. I was clearly panicked by the whole experience as a man stopped me on my way out before I told him my tale. He just smiled and said, 'we get that a lot'.

Nichola's tale is certainly a fascinating one and ties in with other accounts of alleged paranormal phenomena. The fact that she's an American would suggest her prior knowledge of the area was minimal, although it is possible that family members told her the legends before her visit.

A rational mind could point out two key factors in Nichola's story. Firstly, she admitted envisioning living in the hall in times gone by and there are certainly enough trigger objects in the place to enable the mind to be carried away.

Secondly, she stated that she saw the children from the corner of her eye and therefore, would it be unreasonable to suggest something else had caught her peripheral vision and she mistook it for the ghostly children?

As with any location such as this, suggestion is all around and it might simply be that certain people can be so enthralled by their visit, that their minds create what they perceive to be a paranormal experience. That, of course, is not to say her account is false.

It's quite possible that Anne truly did haunt Burton Agnes Hall and that she may be among other similar phantoms, trapped for eternity within the beautiful, yet eerie building.

To this day, there are reports of ghostly figures wandering the hall, children's laughter in the dining room and numerous light anomalies that are captured on a regular basis, and these certainly make you question if Anne truly does haunt Burton Agnes Hall and if so, is her head is still sealed within the walls to this day?

West Yorkshire

30 East Drive, Pontefract

You couldn't possibly begin a paranormal adventure across West Yorkshire without starting at a location commonly thought to be the most haunted house in Europe.

The 1950s-built, semi-detached house on East Drive has been empty for over ten years, the last occupant, Jean Pritchard, having lived alone with 'Fred', one of the most violent poltergeists on record, for almost two decades.

When the Pritchard family moved in during the 1960s, the council house was a relatively new build and was as normal as any other situated upon East Drive. For a while, the family lived in relative calm until Philip and Diane entered their teens.

The first reported phenomena within the house were witnessed by 15-year-old Philip Pritchard and his grandmother. They claimed that chalk dust was seen to be falling out of thin air, at around the shoulder height of an average man. This was quickly followed by water mysteriously appearing in patches across the kitchen floor before intensifying even more as the tap water was replaced by a thick green slime thought, by some, to have been ectoplasm, that oozed from various taps around the house.

As if the experience wasn't bad enough for the Pritchards, the mysterious entity soon became violent and began to throw objects around the room before allegedly shifting a solid oak cabinet right across the floor.

Amidst the phenomena, family photographs were reportedly clawed and scratched, and numerous fires were started in various rooms that were extinguished before any real damage occurred. The petrified family called in an exorcist to rid the home of the entity within, but as the ritual was being carried out, a candle was said to float up in front of the exorcist's eyes before pushing him down the stairs.

The family's nightmare continued as the poltergeist turned its attention to their young daughter Diane, who was just 13 years of age at the time. Not only did the terrified child wake up with scratches and bite marks all over her, her covers were violently pulled away from her in the dead of night and she was slapped across the face numerous times by an invisible presence, the violence peaking when Diane was seen being dragged up the stairs by an unseen entity.

The house is phenomenal, there's no doubt about that. Numerous unexplainable cold spots can be felt and recorded and there is a real sense of evil and depression surrounding the now 70-year-old council house. The current owner claims that he had to take the knives out of the house that is now a macabre tourist attraction, as they kept mysteriously materialising around the house, particularly on the stairs.

Unusually, every single room in this whole house has been subjected to some phenomena at one time or another. The kitchen is reportedly home to strange knocks and bangs and the cupboards have been seen to fly open before slamming shut on many separate occasions. The small coal house is a place where people claim to have been locked in by an unseen presence.

Some even claim that the spirit manifested within the small enclosure, but given the folklore surrounding 30 East Drive, combined with the pitch blackness of the room, are these claims more likely the work of over-imaginative visitors?

In the main bedroom, strange growling noises can be heard, and bizarrely, the tall terrifying figure of a monk has been witnessed by the bed. Door handles and furniture regularly move by themselves in every room and the house contains a definite eerie feeling of being watched.

The small bed in the smallest room has been thrown upward with such force that it was broken and had to be rebuilt. Indeed, the power of the entity is such that one group recently witnessed a bang of such force that the whole house shook, leaving the lampshade in the kitchen swinging, and converting a couple of renowned sceptics into firm believers in the paranormal.

Almost sixty years after the Pritchards were first subjected to some of the most spectacular poltergeist events on record, it would seem that 'it' is still very much in residence – if the hundreds of stories, eyewitnesses' accounts, photos, videos, recordings etc. on the 30EastDrive.com website are to be believed.

The current owner refuses to enter the mysterious property after dark and believes wholeheartedly in the alleged phenomena that reside within the walls of 30 East Drive, but if you are brave enough perhaps you could join one of the many overnight investigations that take place here.

Hall Lane, Leeds

Over the years, a regular Black Dog sighting has been reported on Hall Lane in Leeds, just short of Cookridge Hall, which was built in the seventeenth century.

The Hall Lane 'Shuck', as it is known, has been seen over thirty times along the rural stretch of road heading towards Cookridge. Each time the story differs in account and I've chosen two to share with you that really showcase the polar opposite legends of this mysterious beast.

The first is from Mark Roebuck, a local factory manager and keen cyclist. Mark was born in Wakefield and moved to Leeds when he was 6 years old and has lived there ever since. His account is in his own words and has not been edited:

It was the strangest thing. I used to cycle most evenings and I'd often find myself on Hall Lane. It was a nice stretch of road with fields on one side and thin woodland on the other. Back then, there were fewer cars around so cycling along that unlit stretch was enjoyable.

It was a Friday evening, about 7.30 p.m., and I was returning home after a 15-mile cycle. I stopped for a drink of water as I was only just starting out with my new hobby and I wasn't as fit as I am now.

I remember hearing a strange rustling in the trees and then out popped this enormous dog. It was huge in size, well over half the size of me, and it had long wet shaggy hair and really dark eyes. The strange thing was, I've never really been a dog lover but there was something about this animal that I instantly adored.

I felt a strange sense of déjà vu as if I'd encountered him before. He ran straight up to me and rubbed up against my legs in the way you'd expect a cat to. I fussed him before getting back on my bike, and then he walked by my side as I cycled down the road. As we neared the lights, he bolted off into the trees again and this repeated itself every night for two weeks until finally, one day I went and the dog wasn't there.

I genuinely cannot explain what it was, but I cannot imagine anyone owning a dog of that size. I felt safe and comforted by him and looked forward to meeting him as he accompanied me along that dark stretch of road. I truly felt like he was protecting me but from what, I don't know.

The second tale comes from Jane Hammond, another local woman who works as a nurse at Leeds General Infirmary. As always, her account is unedited:

I used to go out for a run a couple of times per week and sometimes ran along Hall Lane to escape the noise and bustle of the city. One Tuesday evening, I was running along the grass verge at the side of the road, about a quarter of a mile away from Cookridge Hall, when this huge beast of an animal came running out of the trees.

It was barking and snarling at me and had saliva dripping from its jaws. I remember being overwhelmed by its size, as it was almost as tall as me. I screamed in panic and turned to run the other way and it chased after me as I sprinted as fast as I could go.

Suddenly I realised it was silent, and I stopped to get my breath for a second. I reached for my phone but then thought, 'Who the heck am I going to call?'

For some bizarre reason that I honestly can't explain, curiosity got the better of me and I edged back up towards that spot. The night was silent. No cars, birds or people could be heard but I was so fixed on looking for the dog, maybe I just shut them out. As I crept up, I began to think it had run off, when suddenly it came rushing out once more, snarling and running right at me.

This time I fled and I didn't stop. I ran all the way home and was greeted by mocking from my husband. The really strange thing happened the following day when I read in the news that a body had been discovered along that same stretch of road. At first, I thought the dog had mauled someone but, as I read on, it turned out to be a homeless guy that was found and the death was not suspicious. I couldn't help but wonder if the dog had belonged to the man or if it was protecting me from finding the body.

These are just a couple of the stories I have chosen to share with you but in actual fact, there are over thirty accounts in this area dating back to the 1970s. It's also quite possible that there were many more unrecorded sightings before then. I chose these two as they are of the general personality types that would find it difficult to fabricate such tales.

A logical mind could argue that these were unconnected. Perhaps the dog Jane saw did belong to the homeless man. Maybe the dog Mark saw was a different animal altogether that was a domesticated pet out on the loose. Maybe even the size they recalled it to be was nothing more than their imaginations after being startled on a dark rural lane.

I showed pictures of both Alsatian-type 'ghost dogs' and the Irish wolfhound style of the demonic Black Dog or Black Shuck and interestingly, both recognised the latter as the animal in question.

When you take into account the other similar tales, it does beg the question: is a black dog roaming Hall Lane in Leeds? And if so, is it connected to the ghosts that are reported to roam Cookridge Hall?

Are the souls of sinners being collected by the mysterious beast believed to be straight from hell? Or is it capable of protecting certain individuals as Mark claimed it to have done?

The remains of the old gatehouse at Kirkstall Abbey in Leeds.

Kirkstall Abbey, Leeds

These enchantingly beautiful ruins are yet another reminder of the damage caused by the Dissolution of the Monasteries in the sixteenth century. As with so many other eerie ruins, stories of the supernatural are common, yet Kirkstall Abbey tells a tale of a different kind.

These ruins are not said to be the home of ghostly monks or priests from times gone by. The ghostly apparition that is spotted here on a regular basis is that of a white lady, believed to be the spirit of Mary Thwaite.

During her life, Mary was a kind and honourable woman who was most loyal to her husband John. He, on the other hand, was a different breed of man. John was a heavy drinker, a degenerate gambler and serial womaniser during his mortal time on earth. He took his wife for granted, safe in the knowledge that she'd never question him about his misdemeanours.

After the destruction of the monasteries, many people would rummage amongst the ruins in search of any valuable trinkets that had gone unnoticed, with a view to selling them on for a tidy profit. Always looking for more money to gamble with, John visited the ruins with Mary in search of his own fortune.

The folk tale states that at some point during their trip, John spotted another man holding what appeared to be a golden goblet that would have certainly been worth a significant amount of coin. Not wanting the other thief to benefit from the money, John got into a quarrel with the man which ended with a single blow to his head as John thrust a rock into his temple.

As the man lay dying on the ground, John took the blood-stained goblet, which turned out to be little more than a cheap replica, before making his way out of the area as Mary followed close behind.

On their way home, the pair were spotted with the artefact and were eventually arrested for the crime of murder.

Mary was a god-fearing woman and despite the love she had for her husband, she eventually crumbled and told the truth about what had happened that fateful day at Kirkstall Abbey.

John was sentenced to hang for his crime, and with his last breath he cursed his wife for sending him to the gallows and prayed that she would closely follow. Mary was distraught – the battle between the truth and her love for her husband simply did not have any way of ending well. It was said that she spent her remaining years as a recluse, socialising with nobody, before eventually dying alone of a broken heart.

Sadly, even death could not rid Mary of her conscience, despite the fact she had no part in the murder, and it is said that her soul still wanders aimlessly around the abbey ruins, searching for her husband in a bid to beg his forgiveness for sending him to his grave.

There are many witness accounts of people who have claimed to have seen the White Lady of Kirkstall Abbey, often said to be floating delicately around the ruins or through the nearby trees. Others haven't actually seen the apparition, yet claim to have heard her crying or calling out for her husband as she roams in purgatory.

Whilst there are no official records to back the story up, it certainly seems to be a credible one as the actions would have been common around the time, but does that make it true? Or is it just another apocryphal story that has developed over the years?

Parlington Woods, Aberford

If you were to take a leisurely stroll along the signposted Fly Lane in Parlington Woods, you would stumble upon the strangest of trees: a tree that appears to have two legs and almost takes the form of a human.

If then you decided to research the tree, you would discover an even stranger tale and possibly the reason for the paranormal phenomena that is experienced within the woodland to this day. Light anomalies, the cries of a man and a muffled noise, seemingly coming from the tree itself, are just some of the strange things you might encounter.

This tale actually begins in Russia, when Prince Ernestine Vladimir Zmronge was invited by his uncle, Sir Cecil Gascoigne, to Parlington Hall in West Yorkshire for a summer's visit.

The young prince was said to be obsessed by steam train engines and the tracks upon which they travelled, and he was keen to visit the area that was reported to be one of England's finest lines at the time.

For the first six days of his visit, the prince explored the lines, travelling on the rolling stock and inspecting the marvellous engineering before him. On the seventh day, however, the story became rather strange.

Deciding to take a stroll around the picturesque woodlands surrounding Parlington Hall, the prince wandered into the trees and out of sight and hasn't been seen nor heard of ever since that fateful morning. As the prince was of Russian nobility, the police search was conducted on a huge scale, but neither the police nor the volunteers or hounds found any trace of the missing prince. The hounds were also unable to find a scent, although it was reported that many of them congregated around that strange tree.

The disappearance remained a mystery until 1997 when Parlington Hall was torn down, although some might argue it became even more mysterious. As the Orangery was demolished, the workmen found a collection of old papers buried deep within a bricked-up wall.

On examination, they were found to have belonged to Sir Cecil Gascoigne's eccentric wife. Back at the time of the disappearance, hired help on the estate would whisper about Lady Constance Gascoigne and her strange obsession with all aspects of the occult. She was a very strange lady who did not like to be seen within the public eye of the day. Instead, Constance enjoyed reading her strange books of witchcraft and black magic whilst locked away in a private room.

Many of the papers discovered were written in Lady Constance Gascoigne's own handwriting and told of strange spells and ceremonies that were conducted around the tree of the dead, located within Parlington Woods.

The letters alone would have been enough to make this a bizarre discovery, but one letter addressed to the Russian Royal Family that was never sent made the tale even more mysterious.

The letter claimed that on the day of the prince's disappearance he had been wandering the woods, when he stumbled upon Lady Constance Gascoigne and her accomplices during a naked ceremony of witches. The letter then goes on in detail, telling of the anger of the other witches at this man spying on their sacred ritual and enjoying the view of their naked bodies whilst hiding out of sight.

She then goes on to say that the other witches saw the prince and called for Lady Constance to render the young man dumb, so he was unable to tell of the things he'd seen.

The so-called 'Tree of the Dead' as mentioned in Lady Constance Gascoigne's letters.

Upon hearing this, the man bolted off in fear but as he ran back towards the railway line which would help him find his way back to Parlington Hall, another of the witches started a chant of the darkest kind of black magic. Right before their eyes, the man screamed in pain as his legs turned to roots, followed by his entire body becoming the tree that can now be seen.

This tale is by far one of the strangest that Yorkshire has to offer and seems to be too far-fetched to have any truth to it. But if that is really the case, what became of Prince Ernestine Vladimir Zmronge on the seventh day of his visit? How is it possible that such a huge search party couldn't find him or that so many of the hounds ran to that tree? Why did Lady Constance Gascoigne write the things she did before sealing them up in a wall?

With so many possibilities, it is very hard to distinguish fact from fiction in this tale, but the strange paranormal phenomena that are experienced on a regular basis are certainly an interesting factor. Was the young prince really turned into a tree by dark witches practising black magic in Parlington Woods and, if so, is his soul still there to this day?

Steanard Lane, Dewsbury

During the mid-nineteenth century, a young man by the name of William Johnson left the busy mill town of Dewsbury as an outlaw, in search of a new life. As the legend goes, he was the oldest of three brothers and bitterly hated his drunkard father, who had beaten him since birth. The young man rarely retaliated due to the overwhelming fear he had of his father but, on a mild night in May, that all changed.

William's father was particularly the worse for wear that evening from spending the entire afternoon in the local tavern. When he arrived home, he was thrust into a blind rage upon discovering that there wasn't a single drop of alcohol left in the house and, in the usual fashion, he directed his anger towards his eldest son, who was by now 16 years old.

William tried to escape the beating by fleeing the house and hiding in the nearby fields but his father staggered after him relentlessly. As William hid amongst the crops, desperately trying to avoid the flogging he'd surely get, his youngest brother James awoke and wandered into the fields to see what the commotion was.

Upon seeing the boy, their father shouted out that if William was too cowardly to take his beating like a man, then James would receive it instead. As William listened on, he heard the squeals of his younger brother as his father viciously beat him.

William stayed hidden, feeling like a coward, but the cries of his brother overshadowed his fear, and anger became his primary emotion. William found new courage and leapt out of his hiding place, charging towards his father. One blow with his fists was enough to knock the drunkard to his knees, another enough to knock the man unconscious.

Every ounce of hatred and resentment that had been building up over the previous sixteen years all came oozing out of the young man, and seeing his father unconscious wasn't enough for William. After continuing to rain fists upon the man for another minute or so, he grabbed a rock from the fields and finished the job once and for all before tossing his father's corpse in the River Calder that runs alongside Steanard Lane.

Realising what he'd done and fearing the hangman's noose, William bid farewell to his family and set off in search of a new life, changing his hair and clothes and calling himself John Osbourne. For a week or two, he drifted around the area, offering to help out at nearby farms in exchange for a bed and food, before deciding to head south to the magical city of London that he'd heard so much about from his mother.

As William passed back along the spot where he murdered his father, he was stopped by a highwayman who recognised the young fugitive and demanded possessions in exchange for secrecy. William refused to hand over the few coins he had and instead attempted to fight with his assailant. As a knife was produced, he felt a white-hot pain in his abdomen before the highwayman fled the area with all of his belongings.

As the young man lay dying at the side of the road, a spinster stumbled upon him and listened to his tale with his final breath. William 'John' Johnson was buried in an unmarked grave somewhere along that stretch of road within just two weeks of murdering his father. His mother and brothers only discovered his fate a month after his burial.

To this day, people claim to see a young man, wearing old-fashioned rags, wandering along Steanard Lane at dusk. A few people have even claimed to have tried talking to the ghostly apparition before it vanished into thin air. Numerous paranormal groups have conducted investigations into the Steanard Lane phantom, with many claiming to have contacted the spirit of William Johnson through Ouija boards and such like.

It's possible that upon discovering the death of the young man, the case was closed as his body was indeed dumped in an unmarked grave, but with no official records to back up the tale, is the legend simply folklore and if so, who is the spirit claiming to be that of William Johnson? Or is it possible that his restless spirit still wanders Steanard Lane in Dewsbury, as he desperately tries to escape the scene of his crimes and move towards his new life?

The estimated area of William 'John' Johnson's grave.

The area of East Chevin Road where the thunderous hooves can be heard.

East Chevin Road, Otley

If you ever headed out for a leisurely stroll at Chevin Forest Park in Otley, you would most likely end up travelling along East Chevin Road. Each year, thousands of people walk, run and drive along it to visit the location without incident but, for those brave enough to venture out after dusk, it might not be such an uneventful experience.

As the legend goes, back in the early nineteenth century, a young couple made their way along what is now East Chevin Road on horseback. The man was the son of a wealthy mill owner and therefore could never have been allowed to marry the pauper he'd fallen in love with. As they had little option other than eloping, the man collected his maiden on horseback, before riding along East Chevin Road which would then have led them through the forest and away from the bustling city of Leeds.

When the couple arrived at the small thicket that separated the lane from the woodlands, the man, most likely in an attempt to impress his fiancée, tried to jump the gate with both of them on the horse. The animal, unable to make the jump on account of the weight on its back, screeched to a halt and the young woman was thrown from the horse. She smashed her head on a rock and was killed instantly.

The man was so consumed by grief that he took out a small pocket knife and stabbed the horse to death. Then, as he sat weeping by the side of the road, he slit his own wrists whilst cradling his lover's head in his arms. They were found the following day by children out playing in the forest, both victims doused in blood.

Ever since that fateful day, there have been many claims of unexplained phenomena along East Chevin Road after dark. A phantom horse has been reported on numerous occasions, along with the wailing of a woman lost in eternity. The shadow of a man laid dying at the side of the road has also been spotted on various occasions.

Mary Stephenson was a member of a local rambling group. One evening, she and the other ramblers were walking back along East Chevin Road when the whole party experienced a strange event. Here is Mary's story in unedited form:

We'd not met up for a while, so decided to ease back into walking by visiting Chevin Forest Park for the afternoon. We'd had such a wonderful time and a barbeque, that it was quite late when we decided to head back and the sun was all but set in the sky.

I vividly remember walking along East Chevin Road as my friend Sandra was moaning about the sun being in her eyes. It was setting at that horrible angle that almost blinds you wherever you look. Suddenly, we heard the sound of hooves thundering towards us from behind. We turned to look and some of us hopped up onto the grass banking for safety, but there was no horse to be seen, just this horrendous noise that kept growing louder and louder until it was almost right on top of us. Then it started quietening and getting distant as if it had run straight through us.

I researched Mary's story with another three members of the rambling group that I could find and their accounts all matched to the word. Digging deeper into the story of East Chevin Road, I came across Richard and Jane Harrison, a married couple who had been visiting Chevin Forest Park three years after Mary's account. This is what Jane had to say about their experience:

Me and Rich were just packing our picnic things away into our car. We always parked at the Chilli Café on East Chevin Road when we visited which, being locals to the area, was at least once a month.

On that particular day, as we were folding the picnic blanket, we heard a woman crying as clear as day. At first, we joked, but most likely because we were a little embarrassed before Rich said I should go and see if she was okay, woman to woman. I reluctantly agreed and walked along East Chevin Road to the small path that takes you into the park.

As I arrived, the crying stopped and there was no one there. I remember it being deadly silent, not even a bird chirping. I headed back to the car to set off on our way home but, as we pulled onto East Chevin Road, just by the pathway, Rich shouted as we saw a man sat at the side of the road covered in either dirt or blood.

Rich stopped the car and I begged him not to get out but to call the police. The woman's cries had obviously spooked me a little. He said it would be fine and got out of the car but as he walked over to the man, right in front of our eyes, he vanished into thin air. The man, not Richard of course.

Rich turned white and I was screaming for him as he ran back to the car and we accelerated away. I called the police who went out to investigate but later called to say there was nothing to be found. No man, no woman and no traces of blood or signs that there ever had been.

Later, I was telling the story to a friend who told me that something similar had happened to her boyfriend before they got together.

Richard was present at the time and gave constant nods of agreement as she spoke.

The stories I've shared are just a couple of the hundreds that people claim to have experienced, from the strange to the downright bizarre but, is there any truth to the East Chevin Road legends or are they just eerie stories passed on over time?

Perhaps if you look a little closer next time you are travelling to Chevin Forest Park, you might spot the tragic couple or hear the thunderous hooves thudding along that stretch of road as the tragic story is replayed for eternity.

Black Bull, Haworth

The sleepy village of Haworth is most commonly known for the famous Brontë sisters who lived in the area during the nineteenth century. Amidst the articulate family of authors, poets and playwrights, the sisters also had a brother named Branwell who, despite his articulate nature, had a personality a million miles from the rest of his family.

Branwell was both an alcoholic and a drug addict and was much the burden upon his well-to-do kin. He spent most of his days intoxicated within the Black Bull public house, situated adjacent to the old family home.

He was so much separated from his sisters that, after commissioning a painting in 1834 featuring the four of them, he later edited it by removing his own image. An eerie silhouette that almost looks to be haunting the painting is all that remains of Branwell Brontë.

As with most famous families of the past, the restless spirits of Branwell and his sisters are said to wander the streets of Haworth during the evening hours and many have claimed to have witnessed the ghostly figures. The epicentre of the paranormal phenomena seems to be within the walls of the Black Bull, Branwell's second home as it was known.

The ghostly apparitions of two men, always sitting at the same table and quarrelling, are often spotted by guests and staff. One of them is wearing casual attire whilst the other is dressed in finery, including a jacket and a top hat.

Another mysterious entity is often spotted by the end of the bar but some claim this to be the same spirit as one of the aforementioned gentlemen. The apparition appears, taking a drink, before vanishing in front of bewildered spectators' eyes.

Branwell's violent drunken outbursts were no secret and others drinking in the Black Bull back in the mid-nineteenth century were quite used to his temper. It is now believed that Branwell's spirit is responsible for the glasses and ashtrays that are thrown around the bar area by an unseen hand.

His old chair is still located within the pub as something of an attraction, and ghostly footsteps have often been heard stomping towards it before the creaking sound of an invisible presence sitting on the seat.

It was said that, at the funeral of Charlotte Brontë, a mysterious figure appeared to have been standing with the mourners yet no one knew who he was. Could it be conceivable that the Brontë family had indeed always carried this connection with the afterlife?

One very notable account was witnessed by many different visitors on a sunny afternoon. A young girl was sitting with a bag of sweets close to the table where the two gentlemen had been spotted numerous times and, after sitting quietly by herself for some time, she turned and offered some sweets to thin air.

People in the bar asked the young girl who she was talking to and she described a very smart man who had been pulling faces and playing peek-a-boo with his large hat. Is it possible that the girl did, in fact, see the spirit of Branwell Brontë or another entity that haunts this old building?

In addition to the Black Bull, the ghostly apparitions of the entire Brontë family have been spotted around Haworth causing the mind to ponder, are Branwell, Charlotte and their other sisters still haunting Haworth over 150 years after their deaths? Or could it be that the famous story of the Brontë family is so well documented within the history books, that people already know what to expect before arriving at the Black Bull?

Sadly, the pub has closed for business recently following the slump in the hospitality trade. Ghosts aside, with so much history attached to the place, it would be an awful shame if we lost yet another piece of English heritage.

Denby Dale Road, Wakefield

Between Pugneys Country Park and Clarence Park is a bridge that crosses over the River Calder. The bridge itself is nothing unusual, a square concrete structure with red handrails. It's so small that many people would miss having crossed it if they were driving on autopilot. However, the history of the location, combined with the paranormal phenomena that are said to occur here, is anything but usual.

The original bridge was built in the early nineteenth century and would have allowed carriages to cross over the River Calder on their journeys to and from Wakefield. The original construction was made from wood, far more unstable than the concrete structure that stands today.

In 1836, its unsound structure became known in the most violent of ways. A carriage being pulled by four horses was making its way over the creaking overpass when it became unstable and cracked under the weight.

The carriage, along with the four horses, two passengers and the driver were all tossed down into the river that was swollen on account of the heavy rain that had battered the area for some days prior. The four horses and all three souls were drowned in the River Calder on that fateful day.

Ever since then, strange phenomena have been experienced around the location including the thunderous sound of horses, the disembodied cries of men fighting for their lives in the water, and an almighty splash that echoes under the current structure.

I searched for eyewitness accounts and was inundated with the response, all of which claimed to experience any one or a combination of the aforementioned phenomena. During my research, I was introduced to Janet Lowe, a local lady who often walked her dogs along the bank and under the current bridge. This is her story:

I was walking along the river bank on a Sunday morning. It was very quiet, no one fishing or other dog walkers were anywhere to be seen which was strange. I approached the bridge when suddenly I froze as I heard what I believe to be the loud sound of horses running over the top.

Suddenly there was an almighty splash, so loud that I turned and covered myself for fear of getting wet but, when I turned back to the river, it was perfectly still. Not even a swirl on it. I remember breathing heavily and being quite scared at the time, so I hurried my dogs on, neither of which seemed affected by the sounds, but as we quickly exited the far side of the bridge, I heard at least two men screaming for help.

I ran back quickly to where the sound was coming from, the same spot that I'd heard the splash, yet there was no one there. The screams were still echoing around though. I shouted out for anyone that I might not be able to see but within a few seconds, all was silent again.

The water was as still as could be and there was definitely no one around at the time. I was scared by the experience and rushed home as quickly as I could, and it was only later that I learnt of the bridge collapse in the 1800s.

I cannot honestly tell you if I think I experienced something paranormal as in ghosts, but by definition, there was absolutely nothing normal about my experience that day, so I guess I did. I've walked that way for many years since, but never seen nor heard anything out of the ordinary since that strange Sunday.

Janet's story is intriguing and certainly ties in with the factual collapse in 1836. The question is, was she truly unaware of the story before her own encounter? Or did she perhaps already know the tale, even if she couldn't remember having heard it?

Whilst I couldn't find any more witnesses who shared such a vivid experience as Janet Lowe, numerous other people claimed to have heard the thunderous sound of the horses as they ran over the bridge and others claim to have heard the cries of men, drowning in the River Calder.

Whether or not the location truly is haunted, it's a wonderfully macabre piece of history and certainly a very interesting area to stroll along.

Dark Lane, Oxenhope

This chilling ghost story, located at the junction of Keighley Road and the aptly named Dark Lane, just off the A6033, has all the elements of a classic and, whether true or not, the sightings have been reported on many occasions ever since it was first reported to police on a cold September's morning back in 1992.

On that fateful night a local taxi driver, named Darren Cullen, was driving with his wife Diane and their three children in the car. Cullen claims that as he approached the aforementioned junction, a strange shadow appeared in the road and, as the car arrived within 50ft or so, the engine stalled unexplainably.

The family witnessed the ghostly figure that appeared to float about 3ft above the ground as it slowly hovered in the direction of the car. Darren tried cranking the engine to drive his family away, without success. The car had been recently both serviced and tested, and there were no known faults that would have caused any malfunction.

As the children let out a scream, Darren looked up towards the figure to see that it was now directly next to the passenger side window, paralysing Diane in fear. The figure remained for a few seconds before slowly floating away into the woodland and out of sight.

Strangely, with the figure out of view, the car started immediately as the family raced home before reporting the incident to police the following morning. Darren claimed to have seen the entity before but not in the terrifying way as he did on that particular evening. As he had never spoken of it before this however, one would find it difficult to give credit to this assertion.

Since the incident in 1992, there have been numerous claims over the years of similar sightings, although none of these have caused the malfunction of a car's engine. The Oxenhope Spectre, as it is known, is now something of a local celebrity and hordes of ghost hunters and paranormal investigators flock to the location in search of cheap thrills or to uncover what the mysterious figure could be.

It would appear the only certain thing is that the Cullen family genuinely believe in what they saw that night and the whole family agreed with Darren's account. The question is, was it simply mist from the woodlands close by or light fog that caught the headlights, causing the mind to play tricks?

Interestingly, a local paranormal group delved deeper into this tale and investigated the area for four nights in a row. They claimed that during their many seances, vigils, Ouija board sessions and psychic tests, they uncovered the spirit responsible. They claimed that the spectral being was the spiritual form of Arthur Blount, a man who lived during the 1700s and was both a prolific sex offender and a murderer.

I researched the story given by the team with scepticism and, as expected, there are no records of an Arthur Blount living

The location of the regular monk sightings in St Stephen's Church in Huddersfield.

in the area around that time, nor any records of any serial sex offenders or murderers. Of course, I cannot say with absolute certainty that they were incorrect, or dare I say lying, but I'm confident that whatever the spectre may have been it was not what they claimed it to be.

In rationalisation, it's no secret that cars can malfunction for various reasons and perhaps pareidolia played a part in this tale. Or possibly, despite the lack of history that might suggest the reason for this phenomenon, there truly is an entity haunting the area, known only as the Oxenhope Spectre.

St Stephen's Church, Huddersfield

Hidden behind trees, in a miniature woodland in the middle of a built-up urban area, you will find St Stephen's Church. It was opened in 1819 and built by Benjamin Haigh Allen, a local man of great wealth, at a cost of £12,000 – a bill that was paid from his own pocket.

As a highly religious man, it was said that he built the church with his 'blood, sweat and faith', and over the years the building has been used for numerous things, from a refuge during the First World War to a school in the mid-nineteenth century.

The church itself is a beautiful building, very picturesque and set inside aesthetically pleasing surroundings that frame the ancient graves in an oddly eerie yet very fitting setting.

A local folk legend tells of a monk who stopped at the church as he travelled to Wakefield from Bolton Abbey. As the story goes, the monk was attacked by a gang of thieves near to St Stephen's Church and, after being beaten and robbed, he crawled into the churchyard for refuge.

Sadly, having sustained such horrific injuries, he died shortly after within the old church building itself, and now many locals believe that he and two of his brothers reside within the church grounds, protecting it from thieves and vagabonds to this very day.

As with all buildings of this nature, strange tales of hooded figures and ghostly goings-on are rife, with visitors regularly claiming to have seen and heard unexplained phenomena within the grounds of the old church.

Eerie cries, mysterious orbs and phantom monks are just some of the strange sightings reported on a regular basis. One such story that stands out for me was a tale told by Sue Lake, a local lady who worked as a legal executive at a Huddersfield law firm.

Sue told me how she used to regularly walk past the church grounds when out walking with her dogs but, on this occasion, she may not have been alone. She recalls that she was walking her Labradors about 7.30 p.m. that evening when she passed the churchyard as she had many a time previously. This time, however, she felt an overwhelming sense of fear.

She went on to explain how her dogs also acted strangely, both quivering next to her and refusing to leave her side. Sue hurried along the pathway, the old graves on her left-hand side adding to her sense of fear as she walked by the old burial ground. As she got to within just feet of passing the church grounds, she glanced back through the headstones and claimed to have seen the figure of a large man, standing by one of the graves.

He did not look at her and she couldn't make out any details due to the silhouette-type figure caused by the overhanging branches from the trees. Assuming it to be a mourner, she was about to leave when she spotted not one, but two more figures in different areas of the churchyard, all three of them looking down at graves and all similar in build with the same shadowy disposition.

Sue continued to tell me that she could feel her legs shaking with fear and one of her dogs began to growl in the direction of the ghostly figures. Pulling herself together, she was able to continue on her way and, as time passed by, put it down to her imagination. But was that really all it was? Or was there something else lurking within the grounds of St Stephen's Church that evening?

The thing that intrigues me the most about this tale is the information we get when we read between the lines. Sue was by all accounts a highly respectable lady and a pillar of the community. She has a lovely home, a well-to-do family and a respectable job. She was not at all of the personality one would expect to make stories up for attention or gratification.

On the other hand, it would not be unreasonable to logically explain the eerie events that evening. Perhaps her dogs had simply spotted an animal that they were afraid of, causing them both to cower in fear. Perhaps the shadowy figures were nothing more than mourners delivering flowers to a loved one's grave, however unlikely given the time and their description.

Maybe the eerie setting and her heightened sense of fear caused her mind to play tricks on her, and the shadowy figures were nothing more than the shadows of gravestones cast by the moonlight. It's reasonable to think that the headstones could act as trigger objects given the fact she was already spooked. But why now, when she'd wandered this route so many times before without incident?

There are over thirty different accounts of strange phenomena within the grounds of this old building. Orbs have been captured around certain graves on numerous occasions, ghostly figures wander the paths before appearing to walk through the locked door of the church, and a large black dog has also been spotted – which begs the question: were there ghostly figures protecting the churchyard that evening and were they indeed the ghosts of the ill-fated monk and his brothers?

Kirkgate Railway Station, Wakefield

The train station dates back to 1840, with the station building being added fourteen years later in 1854. It remained much the same until 1972 when a series of demolition work altered the old building. Later, many thought it had been a mistake given the history of the place, and in 1979 it became a listed building.

It's a very busy station with commuters and visitors alike, but some of the people using Kirkgate Railway Station in Wakefield might get more than just a train journey.

Over the years there have been many reports of what appears to be a female full-bodied apparition, wandering along platform one or standing at platform two, looking out over the lines as if eagerly awaiting her carriage.

She is said to be dressed in splendid Victorian clothing, complete with parasol. Her dress is said to be of a dome shape at the bottom which would lead us to believe she was sporting crinoline – a metal shape to plump out the skirt area.

The crinoline wasn't invented until 1856, which would date the apparition to beyond that period, but despite the numerous railway deaths that have occurred over the years, I've been unable to place anyone that fits the bill for this apparition.

When one jumps under a train, the impact is so great that it may be conceivable that the soul is ripped from the body and therefore could quite possibly linger in our realm after death, could this spirit be one of these unfortunate souls?

But if she did indeed jump in front of a moving carriage to commit suicide, why would she be spotted at Kirkgate Railway Station? Surely, she'd have done the act in a more remote location where the train was moving at full speed.

Researching even deeper into the history, I was unable to find anyone matching the description or style that had died on the platform either, making this an even stranger sighting.

The ghostly spectre has been reported over twenty times, interestingly after the 1972 demolition work that took place. Could it be possible that this spirit wasn't, in fact, killed by a train-related incident but rather attached to the station in some way?

My research found that the first manager of the station was a young man named Harold Ramshaw, an ex-train driver who had moved over to the administration side of the business.

His wife at the time was Alice Ramshaw and history suggests that she was incredibly proud of her husband for his new promotion and spent many hours within the station that she'd adopted as their own.

This theory seems to make more sense. Perhaps the spirit is that of Alice Ramshaw, wandering platform one to ensure all was clean and tidy. Maybe she has been spotted at platform two, looking out over the lines for the next arrival to ensure the station was running like clockwork.

Given the detail with which this apparition is witnessed, I set about looking for any eyewitness accounts. My own attempts at spotting the elusive spirit were unfortunately unsuccessful.

Amongst the people claiming to have witnessed the spectre with their own eyes, I came across Jack and Wendy Shaw, an elderly couple who were awaiting their train to Leeds in the summer of 2018. Jack was a retired business owner, having sold his successful engineering firm a few years prior for quite a large sum. Wendy had worked alongside him in a secretarial role. This is their story:

Jack: Well, we were just sitting and waiting for our train. It was running late as usual, but it was a glorious day, so we didn't mind too much. Wendy had just gone to get us a coffee from the stall when she came back over, all excited.

Wendy: I was just making my way over to Jack when I saw the most elegant lady on the platform – she looked like something out of a film. She was just walking along, all casual, and looking around the platform. She wasn't with anyone or talking to anyone.

Jack: And that's when she came over and told me. I looked up and there she was. I remember thinking that she might be an actress, on her way to a shoot or something like that.

Wendy: Her dress was beautiful, I can't imagine how much it would have cost. She looked like she was about to get on the *Titanic*.

Jack: Oh yes, very nice. The platform was quiet, only us and a couple of other people waiting for the train. They didn't seem interested in the lass though. Then, she wandered around the side of the stall that Wendy had just bought our coffees from and –

Wendy: She'd gone, vanished. Disappeared into thin air.

Jack: Well, we went around the back ourselves, just to check, like. But she'd gone, where? I don't know.

Wendy: There was nowhere she could have gone. Behind the stall was the train tracks, and she definitely wasn't on the other side.

Following their account, I asked them if they thought it was possible that they'd actually seen a spectral apparition.

Jack: To be honest, it never crossed my mind. I don't really believe in anything like that. Never have.

Wendy: Well I knew right away that she was a ghost. I'm very spiritual you see. I've always had the gift of sight.

Whilst finishing, Jack rolled his eyes and smirked over in my direction. It was quite tough to weigh the pair up in truth, but they seemed genuine and I'm sure they believe in the tales they told. They certainly back up other eyewitness accounts.

Jack excused himself to go to the toilet and when they left, I discovered that he'd paid our bar tab for the meal and drinks, despite only coming at my invitation.

The couple's story is just one of many eyewitness accounts, all claiming to have seen the elusive spectre that wanders the platform at Kirkgate Railway Station in Wakefield.

We may never truly understand who she is or why she still chooses to visit this place. But with so many different sightings, it's a phenomenon that is difficult to ignore.

In addition to the spirit manifesting as a full-bodied apparition, numerous light anomalies have been captured by both CCTV footage and visitors' mobile phone cameras. Strange disembodied voices are reported to either whisper or shout loudly around the platforms and numerous commuters using the night trains have reported the sound of heavy footsteps booming along the platform.

Interestingly, the voices that are heard appear to be male, not female as you would expect given the nature of the apparition that manifests. With that in mind, is the restless spirit of the Victorian lady the only spirit that resides in Kirkgate Railway Station? If she is indeed the ghost of Alice Ramshaw, could it be that her husband Harold is also with her in the afterlife but – for whatever reason – unable to manifest as she does?

Perhaps the spectral apparition is not of Alice at all, but another unfortunate soul. Or perhaps she was the indeed the wife of the original station manager back in the 1840s. Perhaps she died in some way that was connected to the station or this part of Wakefield. Or perhaps, as with the Annison Funeral Parlour tale in the East Yorkshire section, the apparition died before being able to complete her journey and, like Mary Jane

Langley, she returned to her happy memory, only this time one that hadn't occurred yet.

Regardless of the reason, the sightings speak for themselves and perhaps you'd be better off keeping an eye peeled should you ever travel through Kirkgate Railway Station in Wakefield.

Oak Ridge, Wetherby

A haunting on Oak Ridge in Wetherby became something of a cult classic during the late 1990s and proved that not all tales of ghostly goings-on are in fact, accounts of horror.

The current residents of the property wished not to have their address published but were happy for me to retell the tale that had been passed to them from the previous tenants.

As the story goes, an elderly lady in that very house sat in her chair one evening, reading a book in front of the fire. As she immersed herself within the pages, she claimed to have heard a voice, described as that of an elderly gentleman, asking, 'Are you there, Emily?'

Assuming it was the nurse or a neighbour was calling, the elderly lady went to the door but upon answering it, discovered she was alone. Dismissing the incident as nothing other than her mind playing tricks, the elderly lady continued her book before retiring to bed for the night.

At around 3.00 a.m. she was awoken by the same voice, this time speaking a little more. 'Emily? Are you there, Emily? Where are you, Emily?'

The lady is reported to have later told the nurse that whilst she had been somewhat spooked by this experience, the gentle nature of the mysterious voice did not frighten her, despite her unease at it coming from an unseen presence. Once again, the lady checked the house and found she was alone, with all the doors and windows locked tight.

The following morning a friend came to visit her, and she told her of the strange voice. The pair laughed off the story, assuming the book had absorbed her so much that her mind was playing tricks but, whilst the pair were still laughing about it, the voice repeated again. This time it was loud enough for both the ladies to hear it. 'Are you there, Emily?'

At this point, she started to feel uneasy about the disembodied voice and her friend called for the warden who came to the house within the hour to investigate. The warden listened to the strange story and decided to search the house in an attempt to put their minds at rest but, after finding nothing out of the ordinary, the warden left the ladies alone to ponder the situation.

Her friend decided that it may well have been a bird caught in the attic that was causing the strange noise that sounded like a man talking, and set about heading up to investigate this theory. As she looked up in the small attic space, she spotted not a bird or other animal, but a small photograph close to the hatch. It was old in style and probably sentimental to someone.

Seeing such a lovely picture collecting dust, she decided to return it downstairs to the lady, who told her friend that she had never been in the attic. She had moved into the house twenty years ago and she wasn't aware of the picture or the people in it.

The small circular black and white photograph depicted a man and a woman, standing in front of a seaside pier. After some time, her friend left the house, offering to return the following morning to check up on the old lady. That night, she sat once again reading in her chair with the picture close by on the hearth. After an hour or so the elderly man's voice was heard for a third and final time. 'Oh, there you are, Emily,' it was reported to say.

With the many hands this tale has passed through, and the old lady's immersion in her book, it is of course possible that this story is merely the product of imagination and loneliness

– the fact that her husband had died many years prior to the voice being heard gives this theory further merit.

The picture, however, added a nice touch to one of the few ghostly encounters that do not scare, and although the source of the picture has never been traced, nor the people photographed, it is still kept within the house even after two sets of new tenants have taken over the property.

The rational mind could pick holes throughout the story such as why did the voice appear after twenty years if the picture had been locked away in the attic for all that time? There is no unusual history associated with the location that might act as a catalyst for paranormal phenomena.

On the other hand, maybe the ghostly man is wandering the afterlife, looking for his beloved Emily. Regardless, this charming tale brings a smile to one's face and is certainly worth retelling. Its charmingly enchanting and romantic nature make it the perfect story to end our journey across Yorkshire.

Epilogue

We are now at the end of our paranormal adventure across Yorkshire. I hope you've enjoyed reading some of my favourite ghost stories from the county and have been able to come up with your own conclusions and thoughts based upon them.

Whilst the enigma of life after death will almost certainly remain a mystery until such time that we all take that leap into the unknown, my work has shown me one thing for certain: that many people with a belief in the paranormal also have unshakeable faith in it, and no amount of science or reason will alter their thoughts. To my mind that's commendable.

Others do not believe and often do not want to believe and, for that reason, it's more probable than not that they will never consider this world of ghosts and entities beyond what our eyes can see. This could be the reason for these people being unable to come face-to-face with the spirit world.

Finally, there are the people on the fence so to speak, much like myself – people who are open to the concept of ghosts and spirits, but for whom scientific reasoning has to come above all else. That way, when they do eventually see something, there will be no reasonable doubt about the phenomena they have encountered.

Whatever category you fall within, there is something we can all take from a great spooky tale around the fire: entertainment, a thought-provoking topic or further proof in your mind that the afterlife is all around us. So long as it is done in a respectful way to the deceased there is no problem and frankly, I could not think of a better legacy than in 200 years' time, people claiming to see the ghost of Nick Tyler wandering a haunted back road somewhere.

The only thing we can be certain of is that the world around us contains far more than we can currently comprehend, things we are on the periphery of but unable to actually engage with yet. The paranormal is only that because it is something that we do not yet understand, for when ghosts and phenomena become commonplace, the paranormal will effectively be nothing other than just plain old normal, and nobody wants that.

During this book, I've learnt some amazing tales that have excited, scared and humoured me and in addition, I've enjoyed first-hand some of the amazingly rich histories that the fine county of Yorkshire has to offer.

For my own conclusion, I'll say laugh, love, learn and enjoy the topic. But remember, folklore dictates that many of the ghosts were people who had their lives snatched from them, and both their emotions of missing loved ones and the confusion of the new world that they find themselves in contribute to the fact they are now haunting spirits. Your life is still in the palm of your hand – live it!

Biography

Nick Tyler was born in Sheffield in October 1984. He attended Dinnington Comprehensive School and later studied for A-levels in both English and English Literature through the City College of Manchester, where he gained A and A★ grades respectively.

He has shown a keen interest in all aspects of the paranormal from a young age, but it was when he discovered parapsychology at the age of 23 that he really began studying the field. It was also around that time that he started writing, although not at a professional level.

Nick soon learnt that he was able to combine his knowledge of the paranormal with his skills as a writer to create short stories and become an excellent world builder. He dabbled in short stories before moving to novellas, but it was his debut self-published book *Force* that really set him on his path. *Force* was quickly followed by his second novella, *Pendle Rites*, and this time he really found his own style.

When he's not writing or researching for his books, Nick spends most of his time with his partner and three children, visiting places of historic interest around the UK.

www.facebook.com/nicktylerauthor